DAVID
STEINDL-RAST

MODERN SPIRITUAL MASTERS
Robert Ellsberg, Series Editor

This series introduces the writing and vision of some of the great spiritual masters of the twentieth century. Along with selections from their writings, each volume includes a comprehensive introduction, presenting the author's life and writings in context and drawing attention to points of special relevance to contemporary spirituality.

Some of these authors found a wide audience in their lifetimes. In other cases recognition has come long after their deaths. Some are rooted in long-established traditions of spirituality. Others charted new, untested paths. In each case, however, the authors in this series have engaged in a spiritual journey shaped by the influences and concerns of our age. Such concerns include the challenges of modern science, religious pluralism, secularism, and the quest for social justice.

At the dawn of a new millennium this series commends these modern spiritual masters, along with the saints and witnesses of previous centuries, as guides and companions to a new generation of seekers.

DAVID STEINDL-RAST

Essential Writings

Selected with an Introduction by

CLARE HALLWARD

ORBIS BOOKS

Maryknoll, New York 10545

Second Printing, January 2014

Founded in 1970, Orbis Books endeavors to publish works that enlighten the mind, nourish the spirit, and challenge the conscience. The publishing arm of the Maryknoll Fathers and Brothers, Orbis seeks to explore the global dimensions of the Christian faith and mission, to invite dialogue with diverse cultures and religious traditions, and to serve the cause of reconciliation and peace. The books published reflect the views of their authors and do not represent the official position of the Maryknoll Society. To learn more about Maryknoll and Orbis Books, please visit our website at www.maryknoll.org.

Library of Congress Cataloging-in-Publication Data

Steindl-Rast, David.
    [Selections. 2010]
    David Steindl-Rast : essential writings / selected with an introduction by
Clare Hallward.
        p.   cm. – (Modern spiritual masters series)
    Includes bibliographical references.
    ISBN 978-1-57075-888-1 (pbk.)
    1. Spirituality–Catholic Church.   I. Title.   II. Title: Essential writings.
BX2350.65.S7495 2010
248.4'82 – dc22   2010018090

Contents

Sources

BTU   *Belonging to the Universe: Explorations on the Frontiers of Science and Spirituality,* with Fritjof Capra and Thomas Matus (San Francisco: HarperSanFrancisco, 1991).

DTW   *Deeper Than Words: Living the Apostle's Creed* (New York: Doubleday/Image, 2010).

GHP   *Gratefulness, the Heart of Prayer: An Approach to Life in Fullness* (Mahwah, N.J.: Paulist Press, 1984).

GWS   *The Ground We Share: Everyday Practice, Buddhist and Christian,* with Robert Aitken (Boston and London: Shambala, 1996).

LH   *A Listening Heart: The Spirituality of Sacred Sensuousness,* rev. ed. (New York: Crossroad, 1983, 1999).

MS   *Music of Silence: A Sacred Journey through the Hours of the Day,* with Sharon LeBell (Berkeley, Calif.: Seastone, Ulysses Press, 1998, 2002).

WCS   *Words of Common Sense — for Mind, Body, and Soul* (Philadelphia and London: Templeton Foundation Press, 2002).

Other Sources

"Awake, Aware, and Alert," *www.Beliefnet.net* (Summer 2001).

"Enjoying Poetry," edited transcripts of a recording from May 1992.

"Heroic Virtue," an interview in the February 1992 issue of *Gnosis Magazine*.

"O Gaia: Nature and Poetic Intuition," *Epiphany* (Spring 1993).

"Spirituality as Common Sense," *The Quest* 3, no. 2 (Summer 1990).

Some of these and many other articles by Brother David can be found on the website: *www.gratefulness.org.*

Introduction

Someday after mastering the wind, the waves, and gravity,
we shall harness for God the energy of Love, and then for
the second time in history we will have discovered Fire.
— Pierre Teilhard de Chardin

Brother David Steindl-Rast is a landmark figure in a society increasingly aware of the evolution of consciousness gathering momentum all around us — and within. Self-effacing in his personal life as a Benedictine monk, he has nonetheless won international acclaim with his call to grateful living. For Brother David, gratefulness is "the inner gesture of giving meaning to our life by receiving life as gift." He emphasizes that gratefulness lies at the source of the generosity of spirit that the world needs so badly today, thereby "lifting us all in the long journey toward planetary harmony and wholeness."[1] His is a creative response — to be grateful in all circumstances — one he describes as the heart's willing reply to the call of any given moment. It is life lived in all its great fullness.

In 1984, with his first and seminal book, *Gratefulness, the Heart of Prayer,* Brother David began to weave his theme of gratefulness into his writings. Indeed, buoyant pilgrim that he is, he weaves that theme into everything he does. His introduction to *Gratefulness* says it all: "This book is about life in fullness. It is about coming alive." And although he urges us all to "wake up," he notes that "waking up is a continuing process.

No one wakes up once and for all.... There is no limit to wakefulness, just as there is no limit to aliveness." Rooted as always in common sense, Brother David warns that being awake to life is risky: "It takes courage.... We have to choose between risk and risk. We run the risk of sleeping through life, of never waking up at all. Or else we wakefully rise to the risk of life, facing the challenge of life, or love" (*GHP*, 8). Brother David continued to flesh out the practice of gratefulness in a number of his subsequent books including *A Listening Heart; Belonging to the Universe*, written with Fritjof Capra; and *The Music of Silence*.

In these times of upheaval, in the freshness arising as growing numbers of people begin to massively reject the greedy, tawdry schemes of power and the gun, Brother David steadily sounds a bell of sanity — a bell calling us to our senses, calling us to trust our God-given inner authority in the life decisions we are called upon to make.

Growing Up in Austria

Brother David was born Franz Kuno on July 12, 1926, in Vienna, Austria. Hints of Brother David's unfolding destiny, with its generous response to the call of an "evolving consciousness," can be seen in the qualities of heart and courage that Brother David inherited from his grandparents, particularly his grandmother. Equally remarkable was his mother, affectionately known to Franz and his brothers as "The Lion Mother," a tower of strength for many throughout the tragic, chaotic days during and after the war. The fact that she managed to put *anything* at all on the table was sheer magic.

Having known such strong and feisty women so well, it is no mystery that Brother David would have us know that "when I speak of women reclaiming their power, I try to stress that it is their power, since I am convinced that the very concept of women's power is different from that of men. Women's power is the power to foster new life and growth." He goes on to say, "If more people would understand how this life-giving power differs from power over others, the world would be a more peaceful, healthy, and sane place."[2]

Brother David expands on some of his family history:

My maternal grandfather was an officer in the Austrian army and died during the first weeks of World War I. His wife, my grandmother, was an extremely energetic woman — the first woman to ever speak on the radio in Austria — and she conceived a project of shipping war orphans and other hungry children to neutral countries, especially Holland and Sweden.

After World War I, she continued this work under the auspices of the cardinal of Vienna and traveled to the United States to raise funds. When Cardinal Gibbons of Baltimore found out that she had to leave her daughter, my mother, in the care of my great-grandmother while she spent so much time away from home, he gave my mother a scholarship to Notre Dame in Baltimore.... My grandmother continued to spend half the year in the United States all through my childhood. Thus, the pull of the family to the United States was already there when Hitler came to Austria.

Immediately after the war, my two brothers left for the States, and my mother followed not long after....[3] But I was in the midst of my studies and stayed until I received my Ph.D. in 1952.... After my graduation in November

1952, I joined the family in New York, partly running away from a monastic vocation, but [actually] running right into the arms of it, when I visited Mount Saviour in May 1953 and joined on August 20th that year.

By the time Franz was seven years old, his parents had separated. His mother moved from Vienna to a small village nestled in the Alps, taking his two younger brothers, Hans and Max, with her. Franz, already in school, was to stay with his father, but his father, quite incapable of dealing with a young boy by himself, promptly sent him off to boarding school. When Franz's mother heard of her son's misery at that school, she "kidnapped" him, taking him home to his brothers in the village. Eventually, she remarried and lived with the children's stepfather for fifty years, although the marriage was not official because of the church's rules at the time.

Franz was to spend all his teen years under the Nazis, being twelve years old when Hitler marched into Austria and nineteen when the occupation ended. When asked by Michael Toms in a 1991 New Dimensions Radio interview if the experience of spending his teenage years in an occupied country had anything to do with his leaning toward a contemplative or spiritual life, Brother David said "yes." He expanded:

Because Hitler really did persecute the Church...some of our priests and pastors were imprisoned and a few were even executed. We knew that...and that we were in a certain danger if we went to church....For teenagers, [that danger] was exactly what we wanted...so it drove us more and more deeply into a commitment to our faith, and to the Church too.

With all the problems that I find in the Church nowadays, at that time in the '40s, that was where real life was. It was the only thing that you could rely on. I remember, for instance, during the bombings of Vienna, when everything was in shambles . . . and I mean the house, the rooms we lived in, had boarded-up windows because all the gas was gone and the walls had big cracks where you could put your finger in and so forth, and there were no more trains and trams, and at the end there was no more water and no more electricity. . . . The only thing you could rely on was that the priest would come at exactly the same time every day and bring communion, and go through the ruined houses. That meant something. And it continues to mean something to me . . . with all the problems I have with the institution. . . . *There* was the institution at its best.

When I asked Brother David if his faith had been "an expression of patriotism," arising from outrage that his home was under attack, he replied:

There was a strong pride in being Austrian rather than German, and we gave standing ovations to hymns of praise to Austria in patriotic plays (for example, by Franz Grillparzer), which the Nazis permitted in the *Burgtheater* as a wise means to let off steam in an innocuous way. But . . . our conviction of faith went much deeper, and I owe it mostly to that wonderful school run by Catholic lay people, *Neulandschule,* in Vienna. Of course, the awareness of doing something rebellious against the hated government was an additional spice to our faith.

Franz's first love and interest in life was art. In fact, in the same email exchange with me, he says that he "started out as an artist." His father and several of his uncles had been art collectors, and "we often had hungry artists at our dinner table at home. When I was five or six, I wanted to become a landscape painter and was always drawing...also through my adolescence. My interest was definitely in line, not so much in color." Franz's interest in art continued during the war, before he was drafted, encouraged by his friend Uta Guerth, who was a student of Karl Sterrer at the Kunstakadamie in Vienna. "I passed the entrance exam and became Sterrer's student. He had a small class of six or eight students, modeled on the medieval master classes, and we were known as a cell of resistance against the Nazis."

Fortunately, when Franz was eventually drafted into the army, he was never sent to the front lines.

> How that happened I don't know. I just had a great guardian angel, and after a couple of, well several, months — I was there from May '44 until February '45 — I just took off and my mother hid me and two others, one other soldier, at home. It was very brave of her. We were hidden there from February until April.[4]

Today he speaks of his time in the army "as almost a monastic experience": "Hours of marching drill were so many hours of praying the Jesus Prayer, and I felt grateful for this time of undisturbed prayer. Nothing in daily barracks life held my interest sufficiently to distract the mind from prayer."

Surely these practices were signposts on the invisible map of his life, pointing to what lay ahead, as yet so largely undiscerned. Perhaps, too, the discipline he encountered in the army was to contribute to his later conviction that it is our Christian duty to question authority. Indeed, the lesson of the war — to constantly ask, "Who said that and why?" — would remain with him throughout his life. He remembers:

> Our outfit was the 86th Regiment, a unit of "Pioneers" — the corps of engineers. I remember that number, because one of the humiliations we had to undergo when making mistakes was this: we had to climb on our locker, crouch in the narrow space between the top of the locker and the ceiling, and yell 86 times, "I am an ugly little dwarf!"

Perhaps, too, we see intimations of Brother David's later focus on gratitude and surprise in his remark, "On the whole, however, my time at Krems was bathed in gratitude for not yet being dead — a gift surprisingly renewed with every day one was not shipped off."

After the war had officially ended, but before things returned to normal in Vienna, Franz found himself working with refugees some fifty kilometers north of the city on the Czech border. On one of his visits to his Uncle Hans — which always yielded, besides something edible, news from the larger world — he learned that Cardinal Innitzer, archbishop of Vienna, was appealing to young people to volunteer their help to the thousands of refugees pouring into Austria in the area of Laa and thereabouts. The misery was said to be heartbreaking. In his memories of that time, Brother David notes the following:

> That only active love can bring order out of chaos was not a far-fetched idea under the circumstances. It wasn't mere theory for us. To suspend our Greek lessons and respond to the Cardinal's appeal made good sense. An

organizational structure for this venture didn't exist. We
had to...set it up as we went along.... We decided to
break up into groups of two or three, only the men at first,
and walk north to check what we might find...and how
we might be able to help. In retrospect, how completely
unstructured and unorganized this undertaking was [still]
amazes me. But, at the time, we simply took it for granted.

In a journal found later, Annemarie Heidinger, a young refugee
fleeing across the border of what had been Czechoslovakia,
writes:

June 5th, 1945: Old people stood along the edge of the road,
mostly near collapse, because they lacked the strength to go
on living. No one was around to care for them. They simply
died and were left lying there. Was no one burying them?
Or at least covering them with earth? How many skeletons
would the farmers plowing their fields find later on? Here
an arm, there a shoe, there a cracked and fractured skull...

We were dependent upon begging. On one such begging
expedition where I was fortunate to get several slices of
bread and a little milk for my mother...

You must imagine...the road...lined with destroyed
tanks, bombed houses, rotting corpses of horses and graves
...only lightly covered with...earth. A gentle hand had
sometimes laid a flower on a grave.... Again and again,
when my courage failed me, or when something terribly
shocking happened, someone took me by the hand. Strange
how I then regained my courage and strength.

This time it was a young student, Franz Kuno von
Steindl-Rast. In the framework of the Catholic Youth, he
was put in charge of the refugee camp in Wolkersdorf. I no

longer know how many hundreds of people were there. But he managed to comfort and refresh all of these disheartened and despairing people. Sometimes I think of the wonderful miracle of the bread, because suddenly all were nourished and satisfied, and he made us timidly believe somehow in the future.

The numbers of people in the camp slowly dwindled. . . . It became easier to care for those remaining. And now our Franz Kuno performed his miracles. I was naturally extremely happy to meet a person who could speak with me about music, who understood how to talk about the most beautiful spiritual topics, and who carefully, gently, helped me, led me, once more to believe in life, in true life.

On June 23, 1945, that same young woman wrote a letter from Graz to a friend:

Dear Käthe . . . Mother and I are now in Graz, cared for by Uncle and Aunt, my mother's sister. Wolkersdorf was the stopping point in which our situation began to open up. There Franz Kuno von Steindl-Rast from the Catholic Youth Organization brought about the miracle which allowed us once again to believe in humanity. He and his friends provided us not only with food and clothing, but also restored our confidence. . . .

He planted my mother and me in his mother's heart. After much searching, we finally found them in Vienna, and we were allowed to pick and eat cherries from their garden! We "were allowed"! . . . Our conversation with Mrs. Elisabeth was not concerned with need and wretchedness, but rather with the beauty of nature (in their garden) and the positive side of life. A believing human being is the best doctor for a wounded soul! The beginning of spring — of new life.[5]

Many an intimation of young Franz's future work can be seen in these passages, proof that biography is the first clue to theology. We also catch glimpses of that future in the following memories (emailed to me by Brother David), which demonstrate his growing reaction to injustice and his ability to respond flexibly and swiftly to the complex situation facing him once he was able to return to his art studies.

> When the war was over, all those who had been big Nazis went scot-free, and my art professor was scapegoated because, to camouflage his position, he had become a member of the party. Heartbroken, he resigned from the *Akadamie,* and I couldn't find any other teacher whom I liked, portrait painting being my major interest at that time. So I switched over to restoring and became a student of Robert Eigenberger.

Subsequently, Franz became interested in primitive and children's art, although he would increasingly shift his focus to psychology and anthropology, finally getting his doctorate in psychology in 1952. As he put it: "At that time in Vienna we tried to make psychology an exact science, as scientific as possible. We were not the couch types of psychologists but decidedly the rat types. Everything had to be measured. That was my interest, too."[6]

Franz was to weave his interest in art and psychology into the next stage of his life as well, becoming a monk only after he had gone through training in art and psychology and had moved to the States.

Today Brother David still underlines the importance of art and science, saying that while he appreciates what Joseph Campbell calls "the creative interplay of discovery and recognition," for him "the highest creativity in art lies in letting the same creative impulse that brings forth irises and the carapaces of turtles and the spiral nebulae flow through human hands." But he adds:

> This presupposes a high degree of selflessness. Much that calls itself art today looks to me rather like a display of ego, boosted by commercial interests. This together with my growing desire to leave only minimal footprints on this Earth has contributed to my diminished pursuit of artistic activity. In this respect, too, music is the queen of the arts. . . . I like singing — voice or no voice![7]

That love of music is reflected in Brother David's book *The Music of Silence: A Sacred Journey through the Hours of the Day,* first published in 1998. The website which he cofounded in 2000 — a treasure trove of wise words and beautiful images at *www.gratefulness.org* — also conveys that love of music with its inclusion of Gregorian chant in its "Angels of the Hours" segment. Supported by an international nonprofit organization, this website was developed to offer encouragement and new ways of reaching out and "to provide resources for living in the gentle power of the gratefulness that restores courage, reconciles relationships, and heals our Earth." One of its most popular features is the chance to light candles to celebrate or commiserate with friends and family. As of now, over seven million people from 242 countries and territories have sent messages accompanied by glowing candles into cyberspace — a number that only keeps growing.

Answering the Call

In 1953 Brother David, having received his Ph.D. in psychology (with a minor in anthropology) from the University of
Vienna and having followed his family to the United States,
"suddenly" joined the Benedictine community in Elmira, New
York — Mount Saviour Monastery — where today he is a
senior member. While this sudden turn in the roadmap of his
life may have surprised some people, Brother David would
later explain that he had always felt that his move to join
his family in New York was partly a "running away from a
monastic vocation." In Austria, although the question had been
which would come first, "the right girl or the right monastery" — and there had been an abundance of girls — he felt
that the Austrian monasteries of the day, with their layers of
encrusted traditions, had all but smothered the original teaching
of St. Benedict.

The call to a monastic life had clearly remained alive. When
it was suggested in New York that he might be interested in a
newly founded monastery in Elmira, where they adhered faith-
fully to the original rule, Franz immediately jumped on a bus
to see for himself. He recalls that when asking for directions as
he wandered about town in search of a large monastic building, people looked perplexed, until someone finally exclaimed,
"You mean the *monks*?!" Sure enough, he had not found them
because they were living in a farm house. That afternoon while
working on the land with one of the brothers, Franz, reassured
that the community was indeed committed to St. Benedict's
original vision, made his decision. He immediately returned
home, where his mother, seeing his radiant face, burst into
tears, knowing it meant that he would soon be leaving her. Sure

enough, Franz joined the order shortly thereafter, continuing his studies as Brother David.

We recognize Franz's responsive spirit when challenged to a new adventure in that swift decision, so surely made. And that commitment could only have been reinforced when he heard that Father Damasus Winzen, the founder of Mount Saviour, had noted that, "historically, the Catholic priesthood is an anachronistic prolongation of the Old Testament priesthood, which the early Church saw abandoned in Christ," and that his vision of monks was that they served as the "successors of the prophetic lineage." Indeed, before Franz went to the monastery, he would inscribe a book to his brother Max, "From your anti-clerical brother who is becoming a monk." Even today, Brother David points out that many monks have looked at clergy as the "organization men" and at themselves as the "loyal opposition." Brother David recounts that Father Winzen himself used the image of "carps in a pond" for the clergy and for the monks the image of "those pikes one puts into carps' ponds to chase them around so that the moss will not grow on their heads"! In short, Brother David's inquiring mind is never at rest. Take his reply to a recent question about his spiritual reading: "Books on science are on top of my list, and I think of science as a contemporary form of 'exploration into God.' " No false dichotomy between science and religion for Brother David!

Perhaps in addition to that curiosity and openness to surprise, Brother David's responsiveness stemmed from his attentiveness, his ability to experience the fullness of life. Every experience fertilized the seeds of his burgeoning gratefulness for the wondrous givenness of all that is. To Brother David "being" has always implied becoming, and one of his appealing characteristics has been his childlike delight in unexpected surprises.

In late 2008, just back from a retreat in the Sahara Desert, his bemused comment — at eighty-two years old — was, "One thing I never expected to do was ride a camel. And now I have ridden on several!"

Monastic Outreach

Continuing his studies, Brother David accepted a postdoctoral fellowship in 1958–59 at Cornell University, where he also became the first Roman Catholic to hold the Thorpe Lecture-ship, following Bishop J. D. R. Robinson and Paul Tillich. In the 1960s, after twelve years of monastic training and stud-ies in philosophy and theology, Brother David, at the urging of his prior, began leaving the monastery to give talks on monastic life at universities and other locales. He was also encouraged to widen his horizons by exploring the emerging Buddhist-Christian dialogue. Those were busy days.

He met both Thich Nhat Hanh and Thomas Merton dur-ing the 1960s, at a time when both the Vietnamese Buddhist monk and the Catholic Trappist were passionately writing and actively working for peace. In 1995, when Thich Nhat Hanh asked Brother David to write the foreword to his book *Liv-ing Buddha, Living Christ,* Brother David would write about his sense of privilege in meeting Thich Nhat Hanh, known to friends and students as Thây (teacher), and how he recognized in him a brother in the Spirit.

Less dramatic and less intellectual perhaps, but certainly physically demanding, was his participation in numerous Zen retreats. Brother David helped open the Zen Mountain Center at Tassajara Springs, Carmel Valley, in the hills of California. A hot springs resort for over a hundred years, it was bought by the San Francisco Zen Center in 1966. In the afterword to the 2001 collection of essays entitled *Benedict's Dharma: Buddhists Reflect on the Rule of St. Benedict,* Brother David recounts a "surprising little incident" at Tassajara that illustrates how quickly bridges can be built between East and West.

> During one of the first practice periods at Tassajara in California's Los Padres Wilderness, I was a dishwasher. It was a period when we were still working out the practical details of running that Zen Mountain Center. The dishes for scores of students had to be washed by hand outdoors in water from the hot springs and stored on makeshift shelves. When I was asked to leave written instructions for my successor on that job, I did so and added, "Bodhidharma's contemporary, St. Benedict the Patriarch of Western Monastics, writes in the Rule which we follow that pots and pans in the monastery ought to be treated as reverently as the sacred vessels of the altar." A few months later, while visiting a Hindu ashram in New York State, I was asked, "Are you Brother David the dishwasher? We have your quotation from the Rule of St. Benedict posted above our kitchen sink." In so short a time, a passage pointing to the holy ground we share had traveled clear across the continent and from Buddhists to Hindus.[8]

Over the years, Brother David has had many Zen teachers, including Hakkuun Yasutani Roshi, Soen Nakagawa Roshi, Shunryu Suzuki Roshi, and Eido Shimano Roshi. In 1968 he cofounded the Center for Spiritual Studies, and in 1975 he would receive the Martin Buber Award for his achievements in building bridges between religious traditions. He also served as

moderator of the 1996 Gethsemani Encounter. In the foreword
to *The Gethsemani Encounter,* the book describing that gathering, His Holiness the Dalai Lama emphasizes the immense value
of these get-togethers:

> I believe it is extremely important that we extend our under-
> standing of each other's spiritual practices and traditions.
> This is not necessarily done in order to adopt them our-
> selves, but to increase our opportunities for mutual respect.
> Sometimes, too, we encounter something in another tradi-
> tion that helps us better appreciate something in our own.
> It is my hope that readers of this book may find in it inspi-
> ration and understanding that in some way contribute to
> their own inner peace. And I pray that through that inner
> peace they, too, will become better human beings and help
> create a happier, more peaceful world.[9]

Brother David remembers a conversation with Thomas Merton that underlines the truth of the Dalai Lama's convictions.
Brother David had asked Merton whether he thought he could
have presented the Christian teaching in the new, deeper, or
fuller way he now had *without* his exposure to Buddhism.
"Usually," Brother David said, Merton "just laughed off questions like that, not really answering them; but in this case, he
became very quiet and said, 'I'll have to think about that.' Fifteen or twenty minutes later, he came back and said, 'You know,
I thought about your question, and I think I couldn't understand Christian teaching the way I do if it weren't in the light
of Buddhism.' "[10]

While Thomas Merton and Brother David would grow into
their roles as active peacemakers, both were also major figures
in the renewal of religious life. Although both men influenced

many people through their books and speaking engagements, Brother David's outreach probably has had more to do with the development of communities. For instance, Brother David was involved with The Casa in Scottsdale, Arizona, a Franciscan renewal center that held services open to the public. Someone who attended in the late 1970s remembers "the fresh emphasis" on the presence and empowerment of the Holy Spirit, especially through song, prayer, the Eucharist, and loving service to others. She recalls that even a Baptist friend of hers from a staunchly anti-Catholic family used to risk the wrath of her father in order to go to the Sunday evening gatherings — proof to her that these services had something real to offer.

Brother David was also to become a leading figure in The House of Prayer movement, in which Catholics sought to renew their faith through prayer and other spiritual practices after Vatican Council II. The idea, which kindled the interest of many persons reading the signs of the times, was first broached publicly by Father Bernard Haring in 1965 and caught on like wildfire. Within a few years it would become an international movement. Those who speak of it today say that its influence has had to do more with its profound depth of experience than with its numbers, impressive though these are. The movement affected some two hundred thousand members of religious orders in the United States and Canada, as well as untold numbers of lay people.

The Response of Grateful Living

Brother David has written extensively on universal topics, exploring spiritual themes that have emerged as prominent preoccupations in today's uneasy society. To him, the essential aspects of grateful living have always been belonging, beholding, and delight. In his writings he expounds on his major theme of gratefulness, with all its implications for an urgently needed global ethic. He stresses the universality of *belonging* as a profound human need. He speaks of belonging to the universe; to our Earth Household (a favorite phrase originally coined by well-known environmental poet Gary Snyder) with all its humming and buzzing creatures; and to every last one of our fellow human beings, without exception. When asked in a 1992 interview, "What do you see America needing spiritually?" he replied:

> What is most urgently needed in American spirituality today is an ecological awakening. That would be the most appropriate religious gesture for today. It would require all the virtues that religion implies — faith, hope, love, sacrifice — and it's urgent. Unless this spiritual awakening takes place, we're lost.
>
> The core of every religious tradition is the mystical tradition, and mysticism is the experience of limitless belonging. That means limitless belonging to God, if you want to use that term, but also to all humans, to all animals, to all plants; that's at the core of the mystical tradition. And since the mystical tradition is at the core of religion, that sense of belonging is both ecological and religious.[11]

Indeed, when elaborating on our belonging even in unfavorable conditions — conditions in which, according to Brother David, we should "draw out the consequences all the way to loving our enemies" — he quotes author Elissa Melamed: "When you are in the same boat with your worst enemy, will you drill a hole into his side of the boat?"

"Beholding" is another word that sheds light on Brother David's impact on our world. He helps us *see*! His beholding is vibrantly alive. I hear echoes in his writings arising from the nineteenth-century Jesuit poet Gerard Manley Hopkins. There is a line in one of Hopkins's poems, "Hurrahing in Harvest," which says it well: "These things, these things were here and but the beholder wanting."[12] I also detect understandings absorbed from Rainer Maria Rilke (1875–1926), one of Brother David's favorite poets. Rilke includes his readers in his sensuous calling to see things, to name them...to recognize the reciprocal nature of our relationship to God and to life itself. In many ways Brother David echoes Rilke's love for the things of this world in his insistence that they, we, are what is sacred and in his capacity to see the holy in the ordinary:

> I know that nothing has ever been real
> without my beholding it.
> All becoming has needed me.
> My looking ripens things
> and they come toward me, to meet and be met.[13]

Anita Barrows, a translator of Rilke's *Book of Hours,* which she and fellow translator Joanna Macy called *Love Poems to God,* ends her section of the preface with Rilke's declaration that our greatest summons is really *to see* the things of this world. "We *are* because we are seen; we *are* because we are loved. The world *is* because it is beheld and loved into being. *I am in the world to love the world.*"

Brother David's response to such poetry speaks to his attentive attunement to life in all its aspects. If, as the great

Australian poet Les Murray contends, every religion is a long poem, then perhaps only poets can really be theologians — or at least intuitive people of imagination. Could the unsystematic theology of Brother David itself reveal a truth about the untidy God of surprises — the living God, as unpredictable "as is everything that is alive"?[14]

Of the several poems I know Brother David has written, the one called "Ever Deeper Roots in Love," from *Prayers for All People* (180) collected by Mary Ford-Grabowsky, seems to capture a prayer from his heart:

> You from whom we come
>   And to whom we go,
>   Unchanging love,
> You give us time for change and growth
>   In this time of great change in my life,
> please, give me courage to change and grow
>   and cheerfulness amidst growing-pain.
> Let me take ever deeper roots in love
> Make me faithful without clinging
> And let me remain faithful in letting go.
> Into your hands I lay my life
> And the lives of all whom I love.
>
>   Amen.

True, this is perhaps more prayer than poetry. Yet again Brother David is of the same lineage as Gerard Manley Hopkins and Rainer Maria Rilke. He helps us start to behold, to *see* — things that were always there but which, somehow, we did not see. He writes, "True poetry opens our eyes to what Robert Frost called 'the pleasure of taking pains.' And what is gratefulness, but this playful engagement with life as it unfolds in all its challenges and delights?"[15] Brother David's poem also catches the tension between opposites — between faithfulness without clinging, and remaining faithful in letting go. As Beatrice Bruteau has written, "The interactions of the pairs characterize the vitality of the world,"[16] and indeed, they characterize the life journey of this grounded wayfarer.

"Delight" is another recurring theme running through Brother David's life and writing. He delights in words, colors, and images. In his book *A Listening Heart* (22), he writes about watching "a bumblebee tussle and tumble about in the silky recesses of a peony blossom, reveling . . . with total absorption of all its senses in this peony world, performing what is both vital task and ecstatic play." For Brother David, his own pleasure in words, in poetry, his passion for "root-truth in language" — as Roshi Joan Halifax puts it — as he tussles with the meaning at the heart of things, is truly both "vital task and ecstatic play." This man is buoyantly in love with life. As he explains it, "A sound intuition tells us: delight deserves first place and renunciation itself is merely a means for greater, more genuine delight."[17]

Today, as stock prices tumble around us and jobs are lost by the thousands, it is not unusual to hear frugality spoken of in terms of a necessary restraint. But to hear Brother David use the word is quite a different experience. He speaks of frugality with delight, almost as though he could taste it, as a quality that enhances the taste of life itself, as salt flavors our food. His attitude is somewhat reminiscent of that of Bernard of Clairvaux — an ascetic if there ever was one — who put at the top of a list of the benefits of fasting: "Food tastes so much more delicious when you are hungry" (see *LH,* 52–53). Yet at one conference, Brother David was genuinely taken aback to see that some people listening to him were reacting with dismay to his notion of frugality.

But could the participants' dismay actually have underscored their own reluctance to embrace the total self-giving that called for? Yet is that self-giving not the road to delight?

Perhaps their reaction was similar to Brother David's own when he first went looking for synonyms for asceticism and found "abnegation, penance, mortification" — nothing but negative terms — at which point he skipped to the noun "ascetic," only to find that the list of synonyms culminated in "self-tormentor." Today, he concludes that the notion of asceticism has been twisted out of shape by an unhealthy attitude toward the body. He expands:

> In contrast I remember gratefully the body image with which I grew up. A ditty I liked as a child sums up the appreciation of the body that was instilled in me; roughly translated it reads:
>
> > A crystal is your soul.
> > It shines with light divine.
> > For this most treasured gift
> > Your body is the shrine.
>
> On Sunday afternoon visits to the Hapsburg treasure chamber in Vienna, my brothers and I had stared in wonder at treasure chests gilded and jewel-studded even on the outside. They shaped my idea of the body as a shrine for the soul and of the reverent treatment my body deserved. This shaped my own view of asceticism.[18]

Echoes of delight can also be heard in Brother David's understanding of spirituality as aliveness, with gratefulness as the measure of that aliveness — a theme that runs through his talks, whether he is speaking to a small group or to large audiences on lecture tours across five continents. He buoyantly gives of himself to all people, whether his audience consists of starving students in Zaire or faculty at Harvard and Columbia Universities, Buddhist monks or Sufi retreatants, Papago Indians or German intellectuals, New Age commune visitors or naval cadets at Annapolis, missionaries on Polynesian islands or Green Berets, or participants at international peace conferences. In October 1975, he was asked to give the final blessing at the five-day celebration marking the thirty-fifth anniversary of the founding of the United Nations.

There is a subtle differentiation in Brother David's use of the word "gratefulness" rather than "gratitude." He invokes responsiveness, rather than just our response, perhaps best caught in the difference between *"a"* response and a self-spending life of responsiveness. He casts further light on this distinction in his emphasis on the associated qualities of aliveness, alertness, and wakefulness. He emphasizes the dynamic growth in saying "yes" to belonging, and speaks of the importance of caring about life itself, rather than our all-too-human tendency to grasp hold of the structures that life creates. As always, his very words are dynamic:

> The great danger...the trap into which one could fall
> ...[is] to conceive of ultimate order as static. On the
> contrary, it is profoundly dynamic; the only image that
> we can ultimately find for this order is the dance of the
> spheres....We are invited to attune ourselves to that har-
> mony to which the whole universe dances....That order
> is simply the expression of the love that moves the uni-
> verse, Dante's *l'amore che muove il sole e l'altre stelle*
> [the love that moves the sun and the other stars]. But

the fact is that while the rest of the universe moves freely
and gracefully in cosmic harmony, we humans don't....
The obstacle which we must overcome is attachment, even
the attachment to our own effort. Asceticism is the professional approach to overcoming attachment in all its forms.
Our image of the dance should help us understand it.
Detachment, which is merely its negative aspect, frees our
movements, helps make us nimble. The positive aspect of
asceticism is alertness, wakefulness, aliveness.[19]

At the Heart of Brother David's Humanity

Perhaps Brother David's greatest gift to the world has been his
quality of heart. Indeed, his human qualities have shone forth
throughout his life, all bearing witness to the central message of
his life: "Spirituality is aliveness — super-aliveness." As we have
already seen, some of those qualities were particularly apparent in his refugee work after the war. In truth, Brother David's
life and actions communicate his theology in the only authentic way possible, through his personality. Take Brother David's
reply at a weekend retreat at the Upaya Zen Buddhist center
with Roshi Joan Halifax, when she asked us all who we would
like to be in our next life and whom we would serve. Everyone had a different image. Brother David's answer was simply
that he would like to come back as a skateboarder and make all
other skateboarders happy! But other qualities of heart, such as
his compassion, humility, humor, a sense of urgency about the
state of the world, are also communicated in his writings and
presentations. Still others are seen in his lifelong love of animals, for example, in his charming word portraits of the cats
he has cherished: family cats, monastery cats, and wild cats. If

it is true that our strongest influence is the one we are not conscious of — not something striven for in order to affect others — Brother David is such a man. His fundamental happiness speaks louder than his words, for he embodies that vision of children, "that integral and naturally poetic vision we all have before reason, the dream, and the dance drift apart in us, and our perceptions flatten."[20]

In many ways, Brother David evokes a strikingly contemporary note when he challenges, both in his life and his works, the encrusted dogmatism that almost obscures one of the most basic teachings left to us by Jesus. When people said of Jesus, "This man teaches with authority, not as the Scribes and Pharisees," they were referring to the way Jesus appealed to the inner knowing and conscience of each individual — encouraging them to stand on their own two feet — something which has never been, and never will be, popular with authoritarian regimes. Today, of course, we might talk about "authenticity," which is a very modern preoccupation. And it is to that particular hunger for authenticity that Brother David speaks with such relevance. He does this partly by helping us to see clearly the false claims of our consumer society — not by a violent stripping away of our blinders, but by leading us to recognize God's "self-revealing." As he explains so vividly in his book *Belonging to the Universe* (29), in which he and Fritjof Capra explore new paradigms in both science and theology, when searching for your authentic self, "the correct image is not that of your pulling away a veil but of the bride unveiling herself for the bridegroom." And that, he says, comes close to Heidegger's notion of truth, connected with the Greek word for truth. Thomas Matus, O.S.B., who was part of that same conversation, adds that the "word is *aletheia*, which means 'unhiddenness' "; in other words, the truth deliberately "unhides itself, lights itself up" — something, he claims, that "we all experience."

To Brother David, this is an understanding that reaches beyond the limitations of rigid traditionalism, infusing traditions with life — an understanding that reaches to the gnawing emptiness of heart beneath the striving for success that our society urges so relentlessly upon us. In writing about the quest for meaning, he emphasizes that our happiness hinges not on good luck, but on peace of heart. His contagious trust in life includes what the Bible calls "living by the Word of God," which he teaches us "means far more than merely doing God's will. It means being nourished by God's word as food and drink, God's word in every person, every thing, every event" (*A Listening Heart,* 3). He also calls for a resilience of heart and spirit as things unravel around us. Indeed, the war had so profoundly affected Brother David that when he heard the line "keep death always before your eyes" in St. Benedict's rule, he knew he could henceforward never live any other way. Life had become a gift, borrowed time.

There are increasing numbers of thinkers studying gratitude and happiness, not only as solace for the afflicted, but as a powerful new awareness arising in human affairs. This is happening at the same time as institutions are crumbling around us. Originally created to foster and protect life, these institutions, when old familiar certainties dissolve and change, too easily lapse into self-preservation mode. But "anything rigid will crumble" writes Brother David. "Anything that hardens has no future." Here, then, is a steady hand offered to those fearful souls who clutch at their pitiful little bundle of beliefs and call that faith. Here is a man calling us all to a courageous trust in life, a man echoing Krishnamurti's call to trust that the river of life will carry us if we entrust ourselves to it.

Brother David has always stressed the importance of our experience, saying simply that if something does not correspond to our own experience, it is not true for us. Indeed, his whole understanding of the ancient Christian tradition of the Trinity, the subtle relationship between the One and the Many has always been expressed in his own experience of "more and ever more." More seeing, more understanding, more gratefulness, and ever more gifts. In Brother David's interview with Ken Wilber in *Integral Christianity,* on August 30, 2008, they agreed that there is an aspect of God, our selves, and the universe that is best described as being ultimately "One," and there is an aspect that is best described as the "Many." And while we may all be looking at (and as) the very same ultimate Oneness, it is our *interpretations* of that Oneness that determine our relationship with the Many. To underline the truth of this, Brother David added, "I am a little concerned that so many people who have discovered the One simply eradicate their sense of the Many, or consider it unimportant."

In Brother David's generous sharing of his own experience with us, he has shown us the way of all prayer, of the great fullness of life, of living gratefully. As we explore Brother David's writings, may we all experience the expansion of heart he invites us to share. May we all choose to allow the world to give itself freely to us, to shower us with the gifts of perception. In Brother David's words: "Nothing gives more joy than when your heart grows wider and wider and your sense of belonging to the universe grows deeper and deeper."[21]

What Brother David has articulated in his books and is still articulating in the written word, in the contagious example of his life, and in the extraordinary outreach of the website *www.gratefulness.org* adds the evolutionary imperative to the unfolding of our lives. As Anne Hillman writes in a recent book, "The desire to love is not just a personal consecration but one sourced in the depths of life itself. This longing and the need of the earth and its peoples are one and the same."[22] Indeed, Brutus's famous proclamation, "There is a tide in the affairs of men ... "[23] rings true across the centuries. And that tide is rising as the practice of grateful living becomes the global ethic for our planet Earth.

Clare Hallward

Notes

1. A quote from Nancy Roof, Ph.D., president of Kosmos Associates, Inc., founding editor of *Kosmos Journal,* a partner of the Global Commons Initiative, and cofounder of the Values Caucus and Spiritual Caucus at the United Nations.

2. Written by Brother David in praise of *Women, Wisdom, and Dreams: The Light of the Feminine Soul,* by Anne Scott (Freestone, Calif: Nicasio Press, 2008), November 15, 2008.

3. Brother David adds: "During that time, however, I traveled twice to the United States: the first time as a delegate of Young Christian Students to an international convention in River Forest, Illinois, in 1948; the second time in 1950 or 1951, when I accompanied the Vienna Choir Boys as a counselor on their tour through the United States. After that, I stayed on as counselor to the Apollo Boys' Choir in Palm Beach, where I did the experiments for my doctoral dissertation on voice expression." This entire quotation is part of an email from Brother David in response to my own questions.

4. This and the following paragraphs are all taken from Brother David's unpublished World War II memories.

5. Taken from a journal and letter written by Annemarie Heidinger for the years 1945–46.

6. Fritjof Capra, David Steindl-Rast, with Thomas Matus, *Belonging to the Universe: Explorations on the Frontiers of Science and Spirituality* (San Francisco: HarperSanFrancisco, 1991), 6.

7. Ibid.

8. Patrick Henry, O.S.B., ed., *Benedict's Dharma: Buddhists Reflect on the Rule of St. Benedict* (New York: Riverhead Books, 2001), 122.

9. *The Gethsemani Encounter* (New York: Continuum, 2003), x.

10. Ibid., 274.

11. Excerpted from an interview with Richard Smoley, *Gnosis Magazine* (Summer 1992): 41–42.

12. *The Poems of Gerard Manley Hopkins,* 4th ed., ed. W. H. Gardner and N. H. MacKenzie (New York: Oxford University Press, 1976), 70.

13. Book one, second verse of first poem in Rilke's "Book of a Monastic Life," first book in Rilke's *Book of Hours,* trans. Anita Barrow and Joanna Macy with the title, *Love Poems to God.*

14. *Music of Silence: A Sacred Journey through the Hours of the Day* (Berkeley, Calif.: Seastone, Ulysses Press, 1998, 2002), xxi.

15. Taken from the introduction to the poetry feature on the website *www.gratefulness.org.*

16. Beatrice Bruteau, *God's Ecstasy: The Creation of a Self-Creating World* (New York: Crossroad, 1997), 19.

17. *A Listening Heart: The Spirituality of Sacred Sensuousness,* rev. ed. (New York: Crossroad, 1983, 1999), 53.

18. Ibid., 46–47.

19. Ibid., 11.

20. From a poem by Australia's leading poet, Les Murray, "Embodiment and Incarnation" in his book of prose, *A Working Forest* (Potts Point, NSW: Duffy & Snellgrove, 1997).

21. *Words of Common Sense — for Mind, Body, and Soul* (Philadelphia: Templeton Foundation Press, 2002), 84.

22. Anne Hillman, *Awakening the Energies of Love: Discovering Fire for the Second Time* (Putney, Vt.: Bramble Books, 2008), 11.

23. William Shakespeare, *Julius Caesar,* Act IV, Scene III.

Acknowledgments

First and foremost my grateful thanks go to Brother David himself, for having the courage to ask me to put this book together. They go also to Patricia Carlson, executive director of ANG*L — A Network for Grateful Living, for her encouragement and help on so many occasions and her prompt and willing readiness to answer numerous questions. Many thanks, too, to Wendy Dayton, for her most helpful editorial advice and encouragement. And a grateful mention to Janet Boeckh for her laborious work in transcribing the recorded interview with Michael Toms of New Dimensions Radio. Fiona Macfarlane, my friend who took it upon herself to free me from earlier responsibilities so I could work on this anthology, you know of my boundless gratitude for those generous actions so selflessly undertaken.

1

Grateful Living

Gratitude runs as an undercurrent throughout human experience at its most vibrant, always and everywhere.

From Introduction to *Words of Gratitude*

That increased happiness is one spin-off of gratitude is fast becoming common knowledge; indeed, it is almost self-evident. But there is more going on here. Brother David seems to have tapped into a song of the soul, into song-lines of an awakening that echo across the planet. This coincides with the crumbling of many old certainties — as though the Rock of Gibraltar had suddenly cracked in two. Institutions once created to protect life spring into self-preservation mode when threatened with dissolution, as so many are today; and in so doing, their original purpose is erased. At the same time, we see a tide of new thinking arising — the promise of change, which is now enlivening so many. But for the change to bear fruit, all of us need to think about what we can do. Grateful living may well be the place to start coming alive, to start becoming aware of "the voices of an awakening humanity," as Anne Hillman puts it in Awakening the Energies of Love: Discovering Fire for the Second Time.

ALIVENESS

Don't ask yourself
* what the world needs.*
Ask yourself what makes you
* come alive,*

and then go do it.
Because what the world needs
* is people who have come alive.*

— Rev. Howard Thurman

It will be helpful to start with an insight that Oscar Cullmann expressed when he wrote, "There is faithfulness at the heart of all things." The moment we stop taking for granted this faithfulness at the heart of things, we wake up. We find ourselves "at the brink of our longing." On this side is the multifarious fullness accessible to our senses; beyond is the simple fullness of its sense and meaning: the heart of all is faithfulness.

Instinctively we must have sensed this from the start. We could not have taken the first step, the first breath, had we not trusted that the world is trustworthy. A spark of trust glimmers in our guts. When we let it shine also in our heads and hearts, it becomes more than blind instinct; it becomes trust in life, trust in the very source of life; it becomes full-fledged faith, the only appropriate response to the faithfulness at the heart of all there is.   —*LH*, 39–40

We receive the same gift under countless different appearances; this gift is opportunity. Opportunity is the gift for which all other gifts are merely packaging. And more surprising still: out of a hundred opportunities, ninety-nine are opportunities to

enjoy — enjoy what we receive. That this surprises us is in itself
a measure of our lack of attentiveness.   — *LH*, 48–49

Once we set out on the path of mindfulness, one step leads
to the next. The opportunity which a given moment offers to
us is almost always an opportunity to enjoy — ninety-nine out
of a hundred times. (This is so important that it bears repetition.) We need to test this claim by our own experience, for
it provides the basis for the next step. Once out of a hundred
times we will be challenged to respond fully and gratefully to
something which we cannot enjoy. This, too, is given reality;
it, too, is gift. Although I cannot enjoy it, will I still be grateful? It all depends on whether or not I have learned to unwrap
the gift-within-the gift: opportunity — the real gift — is always
opportunity to grow.   — *LH*, 50

What our senses are after is sense. The goal of all our striving is
meaning. Only in sense, in meaning, do our restless hearts come
to rest. This end and aim of all our endeavors is also the goal of
every ascetical practice. We need asceticism, because our senses
do not automatically yield sense. When we deal with living reality, nothing is ever automatic. Life demands what no machine
can give: courage.   — *LH*, 54–55

The fact that you are not yet dead is not sufficient proof that
you are alive. It takes more than that. It takes courage — above
all, the courage to face death. Only one who is alive can die.
Aliveness is measured by the ability to die. In peak moments
of aliveness we are reconciled with death. Deep down within
us something tells us that we would die the moment our life

reached fulfillment. It is fear of death that prevents us from coming fully alive.   — *GHP*, 191

Unfolding life is an organic whole with death. To live means to die with every heartbeat and to be born anew, to breathe out with every breath what is old and to breathe in what is new. This demands courage: the courage to let go. Growing is dying into great growing up. Both demand courage. Without courage we can neither live nor die. Courage to live is courage to die and courage to die is courage to live. We need that courage for our senses to die into sense.

This is the meaning of the motto *Memento Mori,* which we find on ancient sundials — "Remember Dying": remember that this is your task, not later on, once and for all, but here and now, again and again. To remember dying in this way is to come alive. Now and then, one of the sundials will read *Memento Vivere!* The message remains the same: "Remember Living!" Awareness of dying belongs to mindful living as the horizon belongs to the landscape. Death is the horizon of life's landscape; sense is the horizon of the senses. The horizon lies always beyond; we can distinguish it from the landscape, but we cannot separate the two. The same is true of sense and the senses. Reject the senses, how will you find sense? Get stuck in the senses and life will be equally senseless. Both of these dead-end roads are laid out by human willfulness. Obedience, the opposite of willfulness, willingly follows the flow of life to its meaning: through the senses to sense.   — *LH,* 55–56

I would suggest that what I mean by spirituality and by spirit is "aliveness." Aliveness is of one piece with life as we know it —

with the aliveness that you recognize when you are breathing and when your body is functioning.

But it goes beyond that. This aliveness has degrees. Don't you know people who are more alive than other people? Most of us would say yes: So-and-so is really alive! Well, does so-and-so have a higher heart rate or a faster pulse? Maybe, maybe not, but that kind of aliveness is not to be measured by your bodily functions. There is something else that we are talking about here. But it is an aliveness.

What kind of aliveness is it; what are we talking about? Interestingly, sooner or later we arrive at the word "mindfulness." In many spiritual traditions that word has been used, and, you see, always then you are speaking about the mind again, but you are not speaking about the mind in its fullness. So this aliveness is a fullness of mind. However, we are immediately in danger of falling into a trap. Mind will then be spiritual, and body will be unspiritual. Many people fall into this trap, and this is a very dangerous trap because with mindfulness — that is, this aliveness — goes something for which we have no word, and which we should call something like "bodifulness." But that suggests to you the opposite of slimming and is not particularly helpful. What I mean by the word is a full, deep rootedness in our bodies.

Think of mindful people: They are rooted in their bodies. They are alive in their bodies. And it's significant that we don't have a word for that, that we just call it mindful. It indicates that there is something lacking; when a word is lacking in a language, there is some insight lacking — the insight that full aliveness is mindfulness and bodifulness, and it's this full aliveness that we are talking about.

Think about a moment of greatest aliveness in your life, a moment of real mindfulness rooted in the body, a moment in which you were in touch with reality. Those are the degrees to which we are alive and spiritual in this world, the degrees of being in touch with reality.

— "Spirituality as Common Sense"

Speaking at a workshop on poetry and creativity at Esalen, California, in October 1987, Brother David said:

Let me say at this point that when I hear "life" and "spiritual-ity" that is for me really the same. Spirituality is a very abstract word, and it's important, it's good, it's necessary to mention. But it means a heightened aliveness. It means "aliveness on *all* levels," that's how I would understand spirituality. It's very good. Spirit of course means "life-breath," and so spirituality means "super-aliveness," if you want to put it that way.

If we encourage people to be more alive — to find the area of their enthusiasm and feed that area then they may gain in vital-ity and then be able also to take in stride the pain and suffering that's part of life.   — *GWS*, 103

In Brother David's book Deeper Than Words: Living the Apostles' Creed *he courageously brings us new insights, both challenging and all-inclusive, bubbling up from ancient wells of wisdom.*

Our knowledge of Jesus is mediated through others. The Christ in us we know firsthand, even if we have never heard of Jesus.

We turn first to this Christ experience. "Love makes blind," an old saying goes. But it is equally true that lovers look deeply into each other's eyes and hearts — so deeply at times they catch a glimpse of the divine in the other. In this experience lies the seed for understanding the true Self as the divine Self. The Bible expresses this by referring to humans as created "in God's image and likeness." That likeness will shine forth all the more splendidly as we come to realize our true identity — the Christ in us. In this sense, one doesn't have to be a Christian to know Christ. You know Christ when you know your Self.

How do we find that Self? To find it is the goal of every spiritual practice, and the method is always the same: learning to live in the present moment. Different traditions have developed many different ways to facilitate this learning process. One example is grateful living. You can be grateful for the past, but you can only be grateful in the present. You can be grateful that you have a future, but you are grateful now. And whenever you are present now, your awareness has switched the Self. As people come to know their authentic Self, they become acquainted with the inner reality that Christians call Christ.

— *DTW*, 47–48

SPIRITUALITY AS COMMON SENSE

T. S. Eliot said, "Humankind cannot stand very much reality." But we can stand reality in varying degrees, and the most alive ones of us have managed to bear more reality than the others. And what we want to do is become able to be in touch with reality, all of reality, and not to have to block out certain aspects.

The fuller our mindfulness becomes, and the greater we become alive, the more we realize how inadequate language is. So we have to do something, if we want to talk about it, that heightens language. And what is heightened language? The heightened possibility of language is poetry, and so I would like to share with you a poem by William Butler Yeats which hints at one of those moments. It sets religious experience in a context where you would not expect it. Most of us have our real religious experiences when and where we least expect them, and in environments where we expect them we are usually disappointed. This is an autobiographical poem ("Vacillation, IV"), and it happens to Yeats in a London coffee shop. This is how he describes it:

> My fiftieth year had come and gone,
> I sat, a solitary man,
> In a crowded London shop,
> An open book and empty cup
> On the marble table-top.
> While on the shop and street I gazed
> My body of a sudden blazed;
> And twenty minutes more or less
> It seemed, so great my happiness,
> That I was blessed and could bless.

So what happens? He doesn't even say anything about his mind or his thoughts; he probably didn't think a thing at that moment. His body blazed with this vibrant aliveness of mindfulness, which is so much more than thinking. His body blazed! And we have all experienced that, or something similar. He says, "It seemed, so great my happiness, / that I was blessed and could bless." He receives something that he calls blessed — significantly a religious term — and passes on. So something flows through him, and that is that spirit that flows through him.

T. S. Eliot says in *The Four Quartets,* also speaking about
a peak experience: "Music heard so deeply that it isn't heard
at all, but you are the music while the music lasts." You are
the music. That means you vibrate with that music, and even
though you might just be thinking of some flute music or piano
music that you listen to, it's the music of the universe that you
are vibrating to. It's the music to which this whole cosmic dance
dances, and that flows through you — and that's your religious
moment. And in that moment you know that you are one with
all. You are the music while the music lasts, simply that.

And that is now the expression of a profound belonging.
So when you are looking for your peak experiences, or your
religious experiences, as you are scanning your memory, forget
about all the other things you have thought here that side-
tracked you — like "my body never blazed," or "I don't like
music," and all the rest. But the one thing that you cannot dis-
pense with is to ask yourself, "Where did I for one split second
know that I belonged, and know it in my bones, that I was one
with all, and all was one with me?" That's the essence, and that
is a way of knowing. It's the ultimate way of knowing, not limited to thoughts, not limited to feelings, not limited to any other
way of knowing. It is the ultimate of knowing, and in this context I would like to share a second little passage. It's from the
Taoist tradition in China, about twenty-five hundred years old,
in a translation by Thomas Merton:

> Chuang Tzu and Hui Tzu
> Were crossing Hao river
> By the dam.
> Chuang said:

"See how free
The fishes leap and dart:
That is their happiness."
Hui replied:
"Since you are not a fish
How do you know
What makes fishes happy?" ...
Chuang said:
"I know the joy of fishes
In the river
Through my own joy, as I go walking
Along the same river."

And that is common sense — common sense in the deepest sense of the word.... And common sense is a basis for doing, a basis for action. In common sense, action and thinking are closely connected. So common sense is more than thinking. It is that vibrating aliveness to the world, in the world, aliveness for the world, for our environment. And it's a knowing through that belonging, and so a basis for doing, because to act in the spirit is to act as people act when they belong together. We all belong together in this "Earth Household," as Gary Snyder calls it so beautifully, and to live a spiritual life means to act as one acts in one's own house where one belongs together.

One more point I would make: If our aliveness is rooted in the body, what happens when we die? We don't have to wait until we die: What happens when we get decrepit? That's really what most of us are far more afraid of than dying. Dying is probably relatively easy; everybody has at least managed it somehow. But to live with this decrepitness, that's really awful, when body and mind begin to fall asunder, as T. S. Eliot says. What do we do then?

Well, I'm at the age where one really has to begin to deal with those things. I can only give you some thoughts that I myself use for my own encouragement. I ask myself, for instance, don't I know people who are very old and physically quite decrepit, and who are more alive than I can ever hope to be? In a sense, their aliveness is now no longer dependent on the body.

We have even in nature this image of the fruit: The bud and the blossom and the fruit are very much depending on the tree as they are growing. But then comes the point when the fruit is really ripe, and it just drops off the branch and has its own life and it has the seed for new life. I don't want to push the parallel too far, but we can see in human beings that this aliveness in the mind is something that is not limited by the body.

You can ask yourself, for instance: When I think of my friend, someone I really love — or think of someone you have never met, who lived hundreds of years ago and means very much to you — if I think of that person, I come alive. That's the kind of aliveness that we're talking about. Now you come alive in every way through something that is removed from you in space and in time, and yet it has this influence on you. You can only reach this friend with your mind right now, and yet that mind connection makes you really alive.

That mind somehow is life-giving also; therefore, I can very well imagine that when this life outgrows this aliveness — outgrows the limitations of the body — when this belonging gets greater and greater, that sense of belonging can no longer be limited to this one little body I have here, and then I have to somehow leave this body behind and all I have is that sense of belonging, but that is beyond time. It's not afterward. I do not expect to go on and on and on. Like before, I'm very happy that it's over, that it's a limitation, a conclusion. But there is something beyond life that simply lasts, that simply is, that I have, that belongs to me.

That would be one way of dealing with it. And all these things may seem to many of us to come so much from below, you know, working out and up there. Doesn't this come from above? Haven't we been told that God gives us life from above, and God is life, and so forth? Well, my answer is, I believe that myself, but how do you know?

This intuitional question — how do you know? — always leads you back to your own experience. What you don't know from your own experience, you just don't know. Therefore, you have to start from your own experience, and my experience tells me that when I am fully alive, in my best moment of total belonging — when my body blazes, when I'm totally belonging to everything — then I also belong to God and to that which anybody called God if they used the term correctly, that ultimate reference point of our belonging. Therefore, in the spiritual experience, in the peak experience, we have also the anchorage for our religious experience.

— "Spirituality as Common Sense"

Common sense tells us there is nothing in our intellect that did not enter through the doors of perception. Our loftiest concepts are rooted in sense experiences.... People who are too fastidious to...come to grips with concepts at their roots are left with notions that are literally "cut and dried...."

We must, of course, distinguish between sensuousness and sensuality.... Sensuality gets so wrapped up in sensual pleasure that it never goes on to find full joy. A life rooted in sensuousness thrives. A life entangled in sensuality chokes and withers.... Healthy sensuousness rises from root to vine to leaf and fragrant blossom.... True joy surpasses mere sensuous pleasure. Without ever rejecting our senses we must go beyond them. Sooner or later, our senses wilt and die. True joy lasts...

For now, let us emphasize this: to be alienated from our senses means being alienated from what is truly human. How is it possible for someone to get trapped in such alienation?...

Our human condition is such that from the start we run the risk of developing a split in our consciousness. This has to do with our relationship to the body. On the one hand, we look into a mirror and say, "This is me," while all we see is a body. On the other hand, we say with equal conviction, "I have a body." How can you *be* this body and at the same time *have,* own, possess it? Obviously you are somebody, yet you know that you are more than just some body.

The taste of wild strawberries, a toothache, or the pleasure rippling all over your skin after a bath — without a doubt, these are bodily experiences. But can you say this with the same assurance about homesickness, faithfulness, or the awe you feel as you look at the photograph of a spiral galaxy, say the Andromeda Nebula, two million light years from Earth and 200,000 light years in diameter?

We humans belong to both realms, the realm of the senses and a realm that goes beyond them. This stretches us. To avoid the tension of this stretching process we are apt to settle for half of our rightful inheritance. Still, our human birth gives us a dual citizenship. Only by claiming both realms as home can we avoid the polarization of our human consciousness. Our noblest task is to make the most of this creative tension. If we neglect what goes beyond our senses, we sink below animals. But if we deny being animals and neglect or reject our senses, we clip the very wings on which we are meant to rise to higher spheres. Unless we claim our dual citizenship and are at home with both angels and beasts, we become alienated from both, alienated from what is truly human; we become — in Christopher Fry's apt image, "half-witted angels strapped to the backs of mules."

—*LH*, 19–20

I see institutions as serving life. That's their primary function, and they must always be adjusted, and at the right time discarded, for the sake of fulfilling it. It is *life* we should focus on and foster, always giving preference to life instead of the institutional structure.   —*GWS*, 52

Every sensuous experience is at heart a spiritual one, a divine revelation. God's Good News comes to us humans first and foremost through our senses.   —*LH*, 18

Realizing the blessing of aliveness expresses itself in humble, down-to-earth ways of service and taking care of details. And that is something we can practice in any walk of life. It works both ways. As we lovingly take care of details, which so easily slip our mind as we focus on the seemingly big things, we grow into that attitude of caring and of tenderness. We have to cook and clean anyway, so we might as well do it lovingly and caringly.   —*MS*, 63

The tranquility of order is a dynamic tranquility, the stillness of a flame burning in perfect calm, of a wheel spinning so fast that it seems to stand still. Silence in this sense is not only a quality of the environment, but primarily an attitude, an attitude of listening. . . . Let us give to one another that gift of silence, so we can listen together and listen to each other. Only in this silence will we be able to hear that gentle breath of peace, that music to which the spheres dance, that universal harmony to which we, too, hope to dance.   —*LH*, 16–17

BLESSING

Brother David often refers to the "blessing of aliveness." He writes about "blessing" as being the most precise English word for the meaningful flow of the life force.

> *I said to the almond tree:*
> *"Friend, speak to me of God,"*
> *And the almond tree blossomed.*
>   —Nikos Kazantzakis

Blessing is a very concrete reality. The word "blessing" is related in English to the word "blood." Blessing is like the spiritual bloodstream that flows through the universe. When we bless something we are returning what we have received to its source. We know we receive life and breath from a source which is beyond us. We haven't bought it or earned it. We are just put here and life comes to us from some mysterious source, and we can give it back. That is like the blood coming from the heart and going back to the heart. That blood keeps on flowing and if we tune in to the bloodstream of blessing the world comes alive. The same thing happens if we cut off the bloodstream or drain the sap from a tree; life withers.

—From an interview that first appeared
in *Sacred Journey,* October 2001

The basic meaning of blessing: to strengthen the flow of the life-source. The words "blessing" and "blood" go back to the same root. So do "blossom," "blade," "bloom," and other words that have to do with swelling life. Blessing is the spiritual lifeblood throbbing through the universe. Blood is alive only as long as it keeps flowing. This is true also of blessing.

An unforgettable image . . . the river Jordan flows down from Mount Hermon and becomes a natural symbol of blessing — life-giving water for parched soil. Nowhere is this blessing of water more striking than by . . . the Sea of Galilee. Its shores are a paradise of orchards, fields, and gardens; its clear water is teeming with fish. From there the Jordan meanders down to another body of water, the Dead Sea. What a contrast! Here the shores are a desert, the water a salty brine, unfit for irriga- tion, deadly for fish. The same water that feeds the Dead Sea feeds that lake that is the life of Galilee. But there it flows in and flows out again; the Dead Sea does not pass its water on. It remains, and stagnates. Blessing that stops flowing becomes a curse.   —LH, 56–57

During a poetry workshop at Esalen, California, Brother David talked to the participants about a morning prayer "parts of which I very much like":

> Giver of all good gifts, you give us space and time
> This new day, in this place, is your gift.
> Make me live gratefully.
> This day is opportunity
> To receive your blessing in a thousand forms
> And to bless.
> To listen to your word in all that I hear,

And to respond in obedience of heart.
To drink deeply from your life,
And to make others come alive.
By radiant smile, by cheerful answer,
And by a secret blessing.

DO-GOODERS AND
CONTEMPLATIVE EXPERIENCE

Brother David gave us a vivid example of a contrast to grateful living in his answer to a question that arose at a Lindisfarne meeting on contemplative values in a technological society. The question and his answer follow:

Q. Can we use the insight that we get in our contemplative experience for transforming society?

A. That's a very important question. It's very interesting. The question is excellent; it's just the way it is formulated [that] is so significant for us, because you see you are speaking about tasting, an insight of tasting, of meaning, and you immediately introduce the idea of using the tasting to do something else. It's a good question, I am not criticizing you — it is very significant that we all think that way. You have just expressed something that is a deep-rooted attitude of all of us.

And the answer is Yes and not only *can* it transform the world, not only *will* the contemplative experience transform the world if we make an effort toward this, but inevitably the contemplative experience transforms the world. Because that particular little part of the world — center of the world, because

every one of us is the center of the world — has been transformed at that moment. So when you have the contemplative
experience, you realize that this little part of the world has been
transformed and it radiates — it radiates out.

And the reason I am so grateful to you for raising that question is this: it is really important that we distinguish, when we
are dealing with doing something to the world, transforming the
world or something like that, we distinguish between two very
different attitudes that one can take in that situation. The one
in which technological society tends to channel us, whether we
are church people or bureaucrats or technicians or whatever,
is first of all to look for what needs to be done and then go
and do it. And translated into service, this characterizes the do-
gooder. Unfortunately, the world is full of do-gooders who are
just so dissatisfied with themselves that the best alibi they can
find for doing something about themselves is to look around
for what someone else needs and then go and do it. And transform the world everywhere. And be very busy and know much
better what the others need than the others know themselves.
So the do-gooders — I am not knocking them — I can't help
expressing my dislike for them, but I have a certain respect
and a certain pity I would say — but the do-gooders end up
by killing other people and throwing napalm bombs on them
because *they* don't know what's good for them, but *we're* going
to show them!

So the do-gooders have done more evil in the world than all
those other people together who just want to have a good time.
Now, there is also a bad way of having a good time! But if
you really systematically and wholeheartedly go about having
a good time you will radiate good time to the whole world,

because very soon you find that you can't have a good time that is really good without everybody else also having a good time. And then you do radiate into the world and you do serve the world and you do go out to others, but that's a *very* different attitude from the do-gooder — very different!

So your question helps us I hope — it helps me, I hope it helps others — to distinguish between those two different attitudes. Yes the contemplative experience, the contemplative values will change the world, inevitably change the world and *ought* to change the world and ought to influence also — and that is a very legitimate concern I hear behind your question — ought to influence the practical values in the world and ought to influence the power structures of the world and all that.

But not in the sense of sitting around and looking at what needs to be done, and then going and doing it as quickly as possible, but by that inner movement of radiation in which you are really basically concerned with joy, with gratitude for life and gratitude also for the opportunity to do something if it is given to you. *Is given to you* — that's a very different thing from rushing around and busying yourself. Gratitude that something comes your way that you can do. And the most difficult thing about do-gooders is that they never do the thing that is obviously here to be done by them but they are always loving the furthest away people rather than their neighbors — they love humanity and hate their neighbors, or something like that! The most important thing is that the do-gooder is in every one of us, so let's curb the do-gooder and have a good time! It seems we are having a wonderful time here and that is going to change the world. The world has begun to change here. Let's rejoice in that!
— Transcribed from a Lindisfarne tape

TRUE TO EXPERIENCE

Brother David has said that "the human heart is made for universal praise" and that conviction, born of his own experience, is given fresh, jubilant expression in his book Gratefulness, the Heart of Prayer. *Again and again, he stresses not only that cultivating surprise will do wonders for our wakefulness, our aliveness, but, even more, that unless a statement is true to our own experience, it is simply not true for us. Both the elements of surprise and experience shine through the following personal story.*

A close brush with death can trigger that surprise. For me, that came early in life. Growing up in Nazi-occupied Austria, I knew air raids from daily experience.... One time, I remember, the bombs started falling as soon as the warning sirens went off. I was on the street. Unable to find an air raid shelter quickly, I rushed into a church only a few steps away. To shield myself from shattered glass and falling debris, I crawled under a pew and hid my face in my hands. But as bombs exploded outside and the ground shook under me, I felt sure that the vaulted ceiling would cave in any moment and bury me alive. Well, my time had not yet come. A steady tone of the siren announced that the danger was over. And there I was, stretching my back, dusting off my clothes, and stepping out into a glorious May morning. I was alive. Surprise! The buildings I had seen less than an hour ago were now smoking mounds of rubble. But that there was anything at all struck me as an overwhelming surprise. My eyes fell on a few square feet of lawn in the midst of all this destruction. It was as if a friend had offered me an emerald in the hollow of his hand. Never before or after have I seen grass so surprisingly green. — *GHP*, 10

PRACTICES

How can we become more grateful? Are there practices that would be helpful? Brother David suggests a couple of possibilities.

Surprise is the starting point. Through surprise our inner eyes are opened to the amazing fact that everything is gratuitous. Nothing at all can be taken for granted. And if it cannot be taken for granted, it is gift. That is the weighty meaning of the expression we use so lightly when we speak of "a given world." What we have mostly in mind when we speak of a given situation, a given fact, a given world, is that we cannot change it. But that can hardly be called mind*ful* (with emphasis on full). What we should also have in mind when we call something "given" is that it is a gift. True mindfulness gets that gift aspect of the world into view. When our intellect learns to recognize the gift aspect of the world, when our will learns to acknowledge it, our feelings to appreciate it, ever wider circles of mindfulness make our world come alive. I have in mind the image of expanding ripples on the surface of a pond. The pebble that started them is the little plop of surprise. As the ripples expand, we come alive. In the end, gratefulness will be our full aliveness to a gratuitously given world. — *GHP*, 25

Why not start spiritual training with a foot bath? In their own way, your toes will start to sing gratefully. Can anyone deny that this is a step in the direction of "life abundant"? — *LH*, 48

AWAKE, AWARE, AND ALERT
Three Steps in the Process of
Living a Life of Gratefulness

An act of gratitude is a living whole. To superimpose on its organic flow a mental grid like a series of "steps" will always be somewhat arbitrary. And yet, for the sake of practice, such a delineation can be helpful. In any process, we can distinguish a beginning, a middle, and an end. We may use this basic three-step grid for the practice of gratitude: What happens at the start, in the middle, and at the end, when we experience gratitude? What fails to happen when we are not grateful? Before going to bed, I glance back over the day and ask myself: Did I stop and allow myself to be surprised? Or, did I trudge on in a daze? To be awake, aware, and alert are the beginning, middle, and end of gratitude. This gives us the clue to what the three basic steps of practicing gratitude must be.

Step One: Wake Up

To begin with, we never start to be grateful unless we wake up. Wake up to what? To surprise. As long as nothing surprises us, we walk through life in a daze. We need to practice waking up to surprise. I suggest using this simple question as a kind of alarm clock: "Isn't this surprising?" "Yes, indeed!" will be the correct answer, no matter when and where and under what circumstances you ask this question. After all, isn't it surprising that there is anything at all, rather than nothing? Ask yourself at least twice a day, "Isn't this surprising?" and you will soon be more awake to the surprising world in which we live.

Surprise may provide a jolt, enough to wake us up and to stop taking everything for granted. But we may not at all like that surprise. "How can I be grateful for something like this?" we may howl in the midst of a sudden calamity. And why? Because we are not aware of the real gift in this given situation: opportunity.

Step Two: Be Aware of Opportunities

There is a simple question that helps me to practice the second step of gratitude: "What's my opportunity here?" You will find that most of the time, the opportunity that a given moment offers you is an opportunity to enjoy — to enjoy sounds, smells, tastes, texture, colors, and, with still deeper joy, friendliness, kindness, patience, faithfulness, honesty, and all those gifts that soften the soil of our heart like warm spring rain. The more we practice awareness of the countless opportunities to simply enjoy, the easier it becomes to recognize difficult or painful experiences as opportunities, as gifts.

But while awareness of opportunities inherent in life events and circumstances is the core of gratefulness, awareness alone is not enough. What good is it to be aware of an opportunity, unless we avail ourselves of it? How grateful we are shows itself by the alertness with which we respond to the opportunity.

Step Three: Respond Alertly

Once we are in practice for being awake to surprise and being aware of the opportunity at hand, we will spontaneously be alert in our response, especially when we are offered an opportunity to enjoy something. When a sudden rain shower is no longer just an inconvenience but a surprise gift, you will spontaneously rise to the opportunity for enjoyment. You will enjoy it as much as you did in your kindergarten days, even if you are no longer trying to catch raindrops in your wide-open mouth. Only when the opportunity demands more from you than spontaneous enjoyment will you have to give yourself a bit of an extra push as part of Step Three.

The Review Process

It helps me to review my own practice of gratefulness by applying to these three basic steps the rule I learned as a boy for crossing an intersection: "Stop, look, go." Before going to bed, I glance back over the day and ask myself: Did I stop and allow myself to be surprised? Or did I trudge on in a daze? Was I too busy to wake up to surprise? And once I stopped, did I look for the opportunity of that moment? Or did I allow the circumstances to distract me from the gift within the gift? (This tends to happen when the gift's wrappings are not attractive.) And finally, was I alert enough to go after it, to avail myself fully of the opportunity offered to me?

There are times, I must admit, when stopping at night to review my day seems to be the first stop on an express train. Then I look back and realize with regret how much I missed. Not only was I less grateful on those nonstop days, I was less alive, somehow numb. Other days may be just as busy, but I do remember to stop; on those days, I even accomplish more because stopping breaks up the routine. But unless I also look, the stopping alone will not make my day a truly happy one; what difference does it make that I am not on an express train but on a local if I'm not aware of the scenery outside the windows? On some days, I even find in my nightly review that I stopped and I looked, but not with alertness. Just yesterday, I found a huge moth on the sidewalk; I did stop long enough to put it in a safe spot on the lawn, just a foot away, but I didn't crouch down to spend time with this marvelous creature. Only faintly did I remember, at night, those iridescent eyes on the grayish brown wings. My day was diminished by this failure to stay long enough with this surprise gift to deeply look at it and to savor its beauty gratefully.

My simple recipe for a joyful day is this: stop and wake up; look and be aware of what you see; then go on with all the alertness you can muster for the opportunity the moment offers. Looking back in the evening, on a day on which I made these three steps over and over, is like looking at an apple orchard heavy with fruit.

This recipe for grateful living sounds simple — because it is. But simple does not mean easy. Some of the simplest things are difficult because we have lost our childlike simplicity and have not yet found our mature one. Growth in gratitude is growth in maturity. Growth, of course, is an organic process. And so we come back to what I said at the beginning: to superimpose on the organic flow of gratitude a mental grid like a series of "steps" will remain arbitrary. When I am grateful, I am neither rushing nor slouching through my day — I'm dancing. What is true in dance class is true here too: only when you forget to think of your steps, do you truly dance.

— "Awake, Aware, and Alert,"
www.Beliefnet.net, Summer 2001

Brother David suggests that when we first open our eyes in the morning, we all practice thanking God for the gift of being able to see. He contrasts the gift of eyes that see with the millions of people who are blind, many because of malnutrition which, in numerous cases, can be traced back to Northern greed and our consumerism.

Every night I note in a pocket calendar one thing for which I have never before been consciously thankful . . . not just one, but three and four and five pop into my mind some evenings. It is hard to imagine how long I would have to live to exhaust the supply.   —*LH*, 48

At the end of an interview on New Dimensions Radio in 1991, Michael Toms asked Brother David to sum up his practice. Brother David replied:

Gratefulness is the key word for all my practice. I like it so much because it is not religious jargon. It is something everyone can understand, and if you practice it, it will lead you to the experience that matters in all spiritual traditions — it's a key thought for Buddhists, Hindus, Sufis, all the great traditions. Pascal said that the really true human is infinitely deeper than the merely human. To realize that potential is the challenge of our time (the challenge of being truly human rather than merely human).

Q: I can hear my listeners wondering what do we do that is different from what we do now to realize that potential?

Brother David: Trust, trust in life, trust that every given moment will be a good gift, and look for the good opportunities in that given moment.

Second, be open to surprise. Don't go into your office thinking, "Oh, I know what will happen there." Or meet your boss
and think, "Oh, I know what he or she will say," or when you
meet a friend, "I've got your number." Look at them with eyes
that say, "Surprise me — and they will surprise you if you are
open to surprise."

And third, belonging. The great Yes to belonging, to knowing
that we are all one. It is not "we" and "they," them and us.
If you live out of that power, you will have a completely new
and new world. Our world is created out of alienation — we
and they. If you approach everyone with the attitude that we
belong together, even people who oppose you, you will bring
something creative out of that situation.

—Transcription from a 1991 interview
with Brother David on New Dimensions Radio

We are never more than one grateful thought away from peace
of heart.　　　　　— "Word for the Day," *www.gratefulness.org*

2

Unveiling Language

When the pebbles collected wet from the shore dry out,
they lose their luster. Sometimes, though, their imagery is
so unmistakably part of a culture in which the flow of conversation glitters with proverbs that they seem to retain
their freshness.   — *Words of Common Sense*, 21

*Brother David's passion for "root-truth in language," as Roshi
Joan Halifax puts it, is apparent in everything he has written.
His painstaking digging for the original meaning of a word
provides us with layered understandings of such key words as
"faith," "hope," and "love," whose meanings have changed so
remarkably through the centuries. When he writes that "when
it comes to proverbs, I am a passionate fisherman," he is not
overstating the case! Brother David's sheer pleasure in words
comes through in his image of a honey bee tussling and reveling
in a peony world. And in truth, Brother David unveils words
for us, revealing their original freshness. For instance . . .*

FAITH

Much of what passes as faith in God is merely a fearful clutching of beliefs and has little to do with its genuine counterpart. Genuine faith is courageous trust in God's trustworthiness.

—*LH*, 40

On the subject of faith, Fritjof Capra and Brother David had the following dialogue as they explored the frontiers of science and spirituality in Belonging to the Universe, *the book they coauthored with Thomas Matus. Both Fritjof Capra and Brother David received their doctorates at the University of Vienna: Fritjof in theoretical physics; Brother David in anthropology and psychology, after a master's degree in fine arts.*

Brother David: The word "faith" is used in many different ways, even within theology. One may mean doctrine, the "deposit of faith" toward which religious belief is directed. That is by no means the primary or most important aspect of faith at all. Faith is also used synonymously with belief. That's not primary either.

Fritjof: So what is the real, the deepest meaning?

Brother David: Faith, I would say, is a matter of trust, courageous trust in that ultimate belonging which you experience in your religious moments, in your peak moments. Faith is that inner gesture by which you entrust yourself to that belonging. The element of trust is primary. Faith is that belonging. But it seems too good to be true, and so we cannot quite entrust ourselves to it. But when we do entrust ourselves to life, to the world, then our attitude is faith in the deepest sense. It's an inner gesture of the kind we mean when we speak of "having faith in someone" or of "acting in good faith."

Fritjof: This exists also in science, interestingly enough. You know that every leap into novelty, every discovery, is an intuitive leap. But there are some scientists who are more intuitive than others. And the most highly intuitive scientists have this kind of faith. It's very typical of them that they somehow know it in their bones that this will lead them somewhere, and they can trust this knowing. Heisenberg, for instance, said that in the early 1920s, people slowly "got into the spirit" of quantum mechanics before they were able to formulate it, and that was a highly intuitive thing. And people like Niels Bohr, for instance, or Geoffrey Chew or Richard Feynman in physics — I know several of them — just sense that this is the way to go, that they will get somewhere. They have an insight, but they cannot talk about it yet, they cannot formulate it. So there is something like faith in science too.

Brother David: Maybe the difference here is that this "faith," at least the way you have described it, is largely intellectual intuition.

Fritjof: Well, if you call intuition intellectual.

Brother David: It has to do with knowing, that kind of trust. You have an intuition, a hunch. While the trust of faith, in the religious sense, is an existential trust. You can entrust your whole life to this.

Fritjof: You see, the two are related. In science, too, there is a shadow of that existential aspect, because for a scientist, a theory to which you dedicate your life, your scientific career, has an existential quality. That faith has an existential quality, not in the broad sense, but it's more than intellectual.

Brother David: Maybe I should not have said "intellectual." What I meant is "noetic." The scientist's "faith" has to do with intuitive knowing, but it still moves on the level of knowing, not, for instance, on the level of morals at all. But religious faith also embraces morals and that ritual in everyday life which we call spirituality.

Fritjof: But there are scientists, and I count myself among them, who want to make this connection now, reconnecting to morals.

Brother David: Now here we have a very interesting point. I was hoping we would get to this. Are you now speaking as a scientist or as a human being who happens to be a scientist? I think when you speak about this broader connection which you just now mentioned, you are really speaking about yourself as a human being who also happens to be a scientist. And that puts the whole thing in perspective. Religious faith addresses the whole human being, as a human being, in the context of other human beings and of the whole cosmos. Scientific faith is a certain hunch that you're on the right track to figure out some question about the physical world, but it doesn't have any intrinsic connection with ultimate meaning or morality. Somebody working on developing chemical weapons may have remarkable scientific faith in the sense of a great intuitive sense of how to succeed.   —*BTU*, 23–26

HOPE

There is a close connection between hope and hopes, but we must not confuse the two. We set our hopes on something we can imagine. But hope is open for the unimaginable. The opposite of hope is hopelessness. The opposite of hope is despair. One can cling desperately to one's hopes. But even in a hopeless situation hope remains open for surprise. It is surprise that links hope with gratefulness. To the grateful heart every gift is surprising. Hope is openness for surprise.   — *GHP*, 202

Giving yourself to the transforming power of "Christ within you" implies self-acceptance. God has accepted you — as you are — because God looks at your heart of hearts and sees His own glory — Christ — reflected as in a mirror. To accept God's acceptance of us makes self-acceptance possible. To accept God's acceptance is also the basic gesture of faith, our trust in the Giver, from whom we receive all, even ourselves. And to accept God's acceptance is also the basic gesture of hope, our openness for Surprise, including all the surprises of our own unsuspected possibilities.   — *GHP*, 157

The more the insight that life is surprising takes hold of us, the more our life will be a life of hope. A life of openness for Surprise. And Surprise is a name of God. In fact, Surprise is a somewhat more successful name than others, though all names miss the mark when aimed at naming the Nameless One. Like all other names, the name "Surprise" fails to name God. But in doing so it succeeds at least in holding our hearts open for the insight that such failure can be success. And this puts us right at the center of the paradox of hope.   — *GHP*, 123–24

Those moments come to mind when life in fullness overwhelms us. We are surprised by joy. No matter how fleeting the experience is we know now the joy of being open for surprise. For a moment we feel unconditionally welcome, and that makes us able to welcome life unconditionally. The taste of that experience awakens in us a passion for life with its sheer limitless possibilities. That passion is hope: "a passion for the possible.... "

Life itself will purify our hope step by step if we live with a passion for the possible. As we go forward, the apparent limits of the possible will be pushed back further and further into the region of the seemingly impossible. Sooner or later we realize the possible has no fixed limits. What we mistook for a limit proves to be a horizon. And, like every horizon, it recedes as we move on toward fullness of life.

This exploration animated by a passion for the possible is, of course, our religious quest, spurred on by the restlessness of our human heart. Hope makes our religious quest what it is. The very notion of quest implies hope. We may start with the definition of hope as "expectant desire.... " There is a healthy restlessness in the quest which hope inspires. Both expectation and desire contain an element of not yet. We see not yet what we expect. We hold not yet what we desire...yet both expectation and desire already anticipate the goal. Already we look from afar for what we still expect. We set our heart on what we still desire. (The word "desire," derived from the Latin *sidus*, "star," suggests hitching your heart to a star.) The not-yet keeps our quest restless. The already keeps that restlessness healthy. How difficult it is to live in the creative tension of hope — the tension between not-yet and already.   — *GHP,* 124–26

As pilgrims we have a goal. But the meaning of the pilgrimage does not depend on reaching that goal. It depends on remaining open in hope, open for surprise, because God knows our way far better than we do. In that knowledge our heart finds rest while we keep moving on. Hope as the virtue of the pilgrim accounts for both stillness and movement. But the stillness in which we "rest in hope" (Ps. 16:9) is certainly not something reserved for those who have reached the goal by reaching the end of the road. On a pilgrimage, the goal is present in every step along the road, because the end precedes the beginning....

The tension of hope...is basic for that quest for meaning that is the pilgrimage of every human heart. Whenever we find something meaningful, its meaning is given already and not yet. It is there, but there is always more to it. One doesn't find meaning as one finds blueberries in some clearing in the woods — as something to pick, take home, and turn into preserves. Meaning is always fresh. We find it suddenly like the discovery of a unique shaft of afternoon light slanting out of low clouds and onto this same clearing in the woods. In its light we can discover ever new marvels as long as we keep looking.

— *GHP*, 130–31

The stillness of hope is the stillness of integrity. Hope integrates. It makes whole.... It resonates through every part of a person's life, making it whole and sound.   — *GHP*, 139

If living from the heart means grateful living and faithful living, it also means living full of hope. Thus hope gives fiber to our engagement in the great concerns of our world today.

— *GHP*, 143

LOVE

We allow the experience of falling in love to shape our concept of love in general. This puts us on the wrong track. Passionate attraction is indeed an important instance of love. But it is far too specific a type of loving to serve as a model for love in general. When we ask for characteristics of love applicable to each and all of its forms, we find at least two: a sense of belonging and wholehearted acceptance of that belonging with all its implications. These two characteristics are typical for every kind of love, from love of one's country to love of one's pets, while passionate attraction is typical only of falling in love. Love is a wholehearted "yes" to belonging. When we fall in love, our sense of belonging is overpowering, our "yes" is spontaneous and blissful. Falling in love challenges us to rise in love. We can broaden the scope of our "yes." Say it under less favorable conditions and draw out its consequences all the way to loving our enemies. Since August 6, 1945, no one can deny that all of us belong together in this spaceship Earth. "When you are in the same boat with your worst enemy, will you drill a hole into his side of the boat?" asks Elissa Melamed.

— *GHP*, 206–7

The Rule of St. Benedict — the "trellis" (for rule is *canon* in Greek), the latticework that has supported Western monastic life for fifteen hundred years — reminds monks that they stand in the presence of angel choirs whenever they chant. And they sing like the angels, who are said to be calling one another, answering one another in never-ending praise. That is also an expression of spiritual life as a whole, which is, in its essence, a life of love, of listening and responding to God and to one another. Love is not a solo act.   — MS, 6

My own tradition has much to say about the life-breath of God within us; Christian tradition speaks about God's presence in our hearts under three headings: Faith, Hope, and Love. These terms point to different aspects of one and the same living reality. But remember — we are dealing here with life. Life cannot be neatly sliced and packaged and remain alive. Faith, Hope, and Love are not three boxes, with specified contents, as it were. Rather they are ways of being alive, aspects of the . . . fullness of life that is our topic.   — GHP, 86–87

CREATIVITY

When Thomas Homer-Dixon launched his book The Upside of Down in Montreal, he said: "Resilience is the new sustainability." He would have appreciated the following story in which Brother David seizes on the word "Resourcefulness" and the creativity of "Making do." May these notions circulate widely in our fear-ridden society, so badly in need of hope, which somehow, despite everything, springs eternal in the human spirit (to paraphrase Alexander Pope who coined the well-known phrase in 1733).

    Brother David was asked to organize the last two days of a workshop on creativity, which had been running for three weeks at Esalen in California. He opened the morning session by asking for a list of single words that would describe what each participant felt best described creativity. Having received quite a long list, he said:

Well, that's a fine spectrum, and it gives us many good ideas about creativity. Interesting to me is that there is one area that wasn't very much stressed. And usually when you speak about creativity what is *immediately* stressed is the area of *talent,* of being gifted and so forth. It's a good sign that you didn't lock into that. But you are also aware that most people when they hear the word "creativity" think of those creative ones who *have got it,* you see, and us not-so-creative ones who *haven't* got what it takes to be creative. Well, over against that mis-understanding, I would very much stress an aspect of creativity which could be called "making do." When you "make do" with what you've got, that's creativity. If you find yourself in a very tight spot on a hike and you weren't prepared to spend the night out in the mountains but you have to, then you show your creativity, or the creative ones show their creativity by making do with what they've got there, and not bemoaning the fact of all the things they *haven't* got.

So very frequently we also find that the outstanding examples of creativity, when we look through history, are people who have had to make do with very difficult circumstances, or even have had to make do with a lot less than other people who are not so creative...who work uphill against obstacles and so forth. So in this context... [*from the crowd came the word:* "Resourcefulness."...]

"Resourcefulness!" That is really the key word, resourceful-ness. Much more than talent or giftedness, it is resourcefulness. It is resourcefulness with the things we have got.

Among the great gifts that we have got, and with which we can be resourceful, are our shortcomings. They are a great gift, not just falling short of something — they are a great gift. Think for instance of Helen Keller, one of the most creative people in human history. Well, imagine if she had not had her short-comings, we wouldn't even mention her. She proved herself as creative as she did by having to overcome those absolutely incredible difficulties and shortcomings, when most of us are not dealing with anything comparable. But yes, our resource-fulness shows itself when we deal with our shortcomings, with the things we haven't got, as great gifts.

— From a transcription of a workshop
on creativity at Esalen in California

REVELING IN LANGUAGE

For Brother David what seems like "both vital task and ecstatic play" is "reveling, tussling, and tumbling" in language for the sheer joy of it!

If you have ever watched a honeybee tussle and tumble about in the silky recesses of a peony blossom, you will appreciate an image Rilke uses for our talk of translating sense experi-ence into experience that goes beyond the senses. Watch that bee reveling in the fragrance of innumerable purple and white and pink petals until, dusted with golden pollen, it finds the source of nectar hidden at the heart of the flower. Watch how with total absorption of all its senses in this peony world the bee performs what is both vital task and ecstatic play.... This is the pattern of our heart's repeated journeys throughout life and of life's quest as a whole.   — *LH*, 22, 23–24

One of Rainer Maria Rilke's sonnets, translated by Brother David, could have been written for today — for the awakened hopes for change across the globe.

SONNETS TO ORPHEUS: II, 12 (STANZA 1)

Desire change. Be enthusiastic for that flame
in which a thing escapes your grasp
while it makes a glorious display of transformation.
That designing Spirit, the master mind of all things on earth
loves nothing so much in the sweeping movement of the dance
as the turning point.   —Rainer Maria Rilke

PROVERBS AND COMMON SENSE

In his book Words of Common Sense — for Mind, Body, and Soul. *Brother David was not exaggerating when he wrote: "When it comes to proverbs, I am a passionate fisherman." After asking "What is common sense?" he goes on to unpack the notion with a liberal sprinkling of proverbs from many cultures across the globe. He has been collecting these proverbs for a long time, not just for their content, but for sheer joy in the lilt of their language.*

You have heard the old saying, "Common sense is anything but common," and there is some truth to it. We don't have to look far to find ample proof; much of what is said and done in our world is certainly not based on common sense. Yet, how do we become aware of this except by using the common sense we have? We do have it; we just fail to follow it. The language we use shows that we know this. A friend may grab you by the shoulders and exclaim in exasperation, "For heaven's sake, use common sense!" Doesn't this imply that you'd have all the common sense you needed, if only you would use it? What is uncommon is not common sense, but willingness to live by it.

Why is this so? What is our problem? Well, when we talk about using common sense it sounds as if we need only apply our mind to it the way we apply a wrench to a leaking pipe; this puts us on the wrong track. Truly to have common sense means no less than living by it, breathing it as we breathe the air shared by all living beings. We must sense what is common before we can think common-sense thoughts. [How] can we expect common sense to get into our heads unless we open our hearts, breathe deeply, and get a sense of what we all have in common?

To witness life-in-common you need only look at some little stretch of hedgerow or woods: how the trees share their bark with mosses and lichens; how the bushes, herbs, and flowers interact with one another; what a complex give-and-take connects them with the soil, its mulch, minerals, and micro-organisms — with insects, spiders, worms, and other creeping creatures, with birds and animals, with wind and rain and sunlight and mist. A vibrant common sense animates the whole.

Let's not make this image too romantic, though. The harmony we find in nature is different from our wishful thinking; the lion is not about to lie down with the lamb — not even the robin with the earthworm, or the cat with the robin. "Food chain" is too antiseptic; it makes us forget the stark facts: living creatures live by killing and eating each other. Nature is one big eat-and-be-eaten. But why not call it a banquet — a wedding banquet, if you will. While creatures feast on others, they mate with their own kind. Every single flower in the meadow is a lavish display of innocent sex in its naked glory — before a cow eats it up. The hum and buzz of it all is the music of one great wedding feast. A common harmony guides the steps of each creature in this fierce but joyful dance of all with all.

All, except us humans. We are the only awkward ones, the wallflowers at this dance. We are unique in nature, and this is a great gift, but it becomes our downfall. We tend to confuse the truth that we are different with the illusion of being separate. This dulls our sense of the common rhythm and makes us fall out of step in the great dance.   — *WCS*, 3, 5–6

Like slick fish, proverbs have managed to slide through the nets of scholars who set out to catch them in a definition. One thing is certain, however: a proverb is a common saying that makes eminent sense to those who use it. The natural habitat of proverbs is in the waters of common sense. They swim with equal ease in the different strata of a given society: "Whoever has a proverb is worthy of attention," the Chinese say, "be it a mandarin or a coolie." They are common to far distant geographic areas, migrating from country to country and from language to language. Not even the waterfalls that separate period from period in history can stop proverbs, and some of them have been common throughout vastly different eras, retaining their wiggling vitality for thousands of years.   — *WCS*, 13

More than two thousand years ago, the Roman scholar Varro wrote, *Non omnes, qui habent citharam, sunt citharaoes* (They are not all harpists who own a harp). He may have created a proverb, or — more likely — recorded one that was already an old saw. At any rate, through Varro it became popular, and its popularity was still so strong a thousand years later that many new proverbs were created on its pattern. "They are not all hunters who blow horns." "They are not all cooks who carry long knives." And, "They are not all friends who laugh with you." The Dutch people were particularly fond of this last one (*Zijn neit alle frienden, die hem toelachen*) and seem to have brought it to the West Indies. There it survives today — another thousand years later in an African American version: "They are not all friends who grin showing their teeth." Other proverbs have had a long life, too. Some fifteen hundred years ago, Plutarch had already quoted, "The wearer knows best where the shoe pinches." His contemporary, St. Jerome, called "Don't look a gift horse in the mouth!" an old saw. He had fished it up from the vernacular, the language of common people, the language into which he was translating the Bible.

When it comes to proverbs, I am a passionate fisherman. Since the waters of common sense flow in every part of the world, we may be lucky and catch the same proverb in streams thousands of miles apart — or rather, find the same insight turned into a proverb by an altogether different culture. In New York, they say, "Every family has a skeleton in the closet." In the West Indies, it becomes, "Every house have him dirty corner," and in the southern United States, "Every cabin has its mosquito." For the Haya in East Africa, it is "Every hill has its leopard," and the Jabo give a special twist to that skeleton in the closet: "Chicken says, 'If you scratch too hard, you come upon the bones of your mother.'" To find the same with a difference is always a thrill.

Even within the same culture, you may find a delightful variety of images to get the same idea across. Which of these four proverbs would you choose to tell someone "You had it coming"? "If you won't stand blow, no play with stick." "One that carries straw mustn't fool with fire." "If you lie with the puppy, you get bitten by the fleas." "One who swims with fish must eat worms." All four of them come out of African American culture with its colorful imagery. There is no better way of coming to know a given culture than to savor its oral tradition of proverbs. Unfortunately, the media tend to make language sterile, and proverbs are becoming an endangered species. — *WCS*, 14–15, 17

In the Austria of my childhood, everyone seemed to agree with the Basque proverb, "Old words: wise words." Or with the English, "All good sense of the world runs into proverbs." Besides, as the Arabs know, "A proverb is to speech what salt is to food." Cicero had already spoken of "salting" his elegant Latin prose with proverbs, and my Great Aunt Jenny, who liked lots of salt on her potatoes, salted the advice she gave us children with proverbs too. The mailman, the gypsies, and the tinker who came to the door used proverbs. So did the pastor, the butcher, and above all our tutor. None of them knew that unimaginably far away, in the Sudan, the Ojai said, "For every occasion there is a proverb." But they would all have agreed that proverbs were "the wisdom of the common people." Everyone believed in the proverb of all proverbs, which was still current among us in its Latin form, *Vox populi, vox Dei* ("The voice of the people: God's voice"). — *WCS*, 17

For a long time now, I have been collecting proverbs, not only for their content, but also for sheer pleasure in their language. I pick them up with the same enjoyment with which I collect pebbles when I walk along the shore. Just as the tides smooth and polish pebbles, daily use shapes proverbs until not one excess word is left...

Pebbles I pick have other delightful qualities besides being smooth to the touch. Their polish brings out the design in the rock. Thus, many proverbs have obviously been shaped and reshaped as they went from mouth to mouth through the centuries, until language has found the perfect design.

— WCS, 19

When the pebbles collected wet from the shore dry out, they lose their luster. Sometimes, though, their imagery is so unmistakably part of a culture in which the flow of conversation glitters with proverbs that they seem to retain their freshness.

— WCS, 21

In one type of proverb, common sense reaches its perfect expression. At first sight, proverbs of this sort may appear homespun — like many great things. In fact, "homespun" is a good word to describe them if we give to "home" its deepest meaning. Common sense is the thinking and feeling and willing that we share with the whole Earth Household. There is our true home, and there the proverbs of this kind have been "spun." They do not philosophize or moralize; they simply hold up one image, as if to say "Look!" And the more we look, the more we see. "Under trees it rains twice" (Swiss). "A tiny needle goes through coarse cloth" (Sudan). "Dead twig shows itself when the buds come out" (African American). "Drop by drop carves the stone" (ancient Rome). These images are spun by the great Mother-of-All on the same spinning wheel on which the threads of the world itself are being spun. This is why these proverbs shine so brightly and yield ever new insights. We find images of this kind throughout the parables of Jesus.

— WCS, 21, 23

THE PARABLES OF JESUS

In discussing the stories that Jesus told when he was teaching, Brother David constantly points out the gap between what is alive and the deadening effect of the slide into mindless repetition, the discrepancies in meaning that arise when we refer to what was later taught about Jesus whereas we need always to refer back to the teachings of Jesus himself.

The original message of Jesus still sparkles with freshness, and nowhere more brilliantly than in his parables. Like grains of gold in sand, these parables were deposited in the earliest layers of Christian tradition. Better than most other gospel passages, they preserve the live words of the Teacher. That Jesus taught in parables is one of the few historical facts about him that we know with certainty. Mark, the earliest gospel writer, even claims, "Without a parable he did not speak to them" (4:34). Though Mark may be overstating his case, the fact remains that we can find the essence of Jesus' message in his parables. This is true in a double sense — with regard to content and with regard to form. Parables contain the gist of what Jesus taught and his choice of the parable form is in itself an essential aspect of his message. — WCS, 25

Many parables of Jesus resemble those proverbs in which a vivid image sparks a common-sense insight. Sometimes expanding the image into a brief narrative, Jesus pushes the inner mechanism of that type of proverb just a little further. Typically, his parables have three steps. Step one confronts us with a question: "Who of you...? Who of you doesn't know that figs don't grow on thistles? That blind guides are not particularly

reliable? That a tiny seed grows into a tall tree?" Step two
is our reply. Without hesitation we answer: "Well, everybody
knows this. Common sense tells us so!" But then comes step
three — another question, and often a merely implicit one: "Ah,
if you know it so well, why don't you act accordingly?" Laugh-
ter is the proper response. The joke is on us. We can all laugh
together at the fact that we have all the common sense we need
yet when it comes to the most important matters, we live like
nitwits. Parable after parable is a variation on this joke.

A closer look will show us, however, that few of the parables
in the gospels still work as jokes. The reason is obvious. How
often can you tell the same joke to the same audience? After
a few times even the most patient ones will boo. And yet, the
images Jesus used remain precious to his followers. So tradition
retains and repeats the images, but turns the jokes into moraliz-
ing stories. The so-called Parable of the Good Samaritan (Luke
10:29–37) is a good example of this tendency.

The context in Luke's gospel is a discussion about loving
one's neighbor. "But who *is* my neighbor?" someone asks. Jesus
picks up the implication, "God forbid that I should be kind to
someone who isn't — in the full technical sense — my neighbor!" He seems to chuckle as he answers by telling a story: "A
man went down from Jerusalem to Jericho . . . "

Now remember: this man is you. The first person mentioned
is often the one with whom you must identify for a joke to
work. So you travel down that road, notorious for its robbers,
and sure enough, one of them holds you up, beats you, strips
you, and lets you lie there half dead. You are only half dead;
this is important, because you must be just alive enough to see
what happens next. This story is told from the perspective of
the one who was mugged, and that is you.

So you lie there by the roadside and someone comes down the same road. "Oh, here comes my neighbor," your heart cries out. "He must help me!" Notice that you suddenly know who is your neighbor, now that you are in trouble. You know it, but he doesn't — or doesn't want to know; he walks right by. But wait, you get another chance. Another traveler is coming by. "Surely this one will know that he is my neighbor and will help me!" You don't know who it is, but common sense tells you that he is your neighbor. Unfortunately, he too walks by on the other side of the road. But don't give up yet (there is always a third one in a joke of this kind). Each time you hope more fervently that the stranger will know he is your neighbor. Finally a third one comes by — a Samaritan. By now the story has maneuvered you into a position where you are more than glad to welcome absolutely anyone as a neighbor. Anyone without restriction? Yes, even a Samaritan! For a Jew to think of a Samaritan as neighbor was outrageous. But here common sense suddenly clashes with public opinion and wins.

Tongue in cheek, Jesus asks, "Now which of the three, do you think, was neighbor to him who fell among the robbers?"

— *WCS*, 27–29

The one who had asked "Who is my neighbor?" can no longer claim that he doesn't know the answer. Still, he will only say, "The one who showed him mercy." The S-word sticks in his throat; he cannot get it over his lips that a "dirty Samaritan" was indeed his neighbor.

The stories Jesus tells are not edifying tales, but jokes of this kind: You want to know who is your neighbor? Wait till you get into trouble. Why does your common sense work so well when you are in need? Why is your sense of our common humanity so restricted when another needs your help?

You notice the three elements typical of Jesus' parables. A strong image: yourself as victim of a mugging; a common-sense insight: when you are in need, you know that everyone is your neighbor; and the point of the joke: If you know this so well, Dummy, why act as if you didn't?

By replacing "Samaritan" with the name of a current ethnic scapegoat we, too, might get the point and laugh at our own prejudices. Of course, by calling this the Parable of the Good Samaritan, we kill the joke. Among those to whom Jesus first told the parable, the only "good Samaritan" was a dead Samaritan. Miss this point and all that's left is an edifying tale told by a detached reporter. But when we look at the events through the eyes of the prejudiced victim with whom we identify, we are suddenly confronted with the authority of common sense.

— WCS, 31, 33

3

Prayer

Prayer is not sending an order and expecting it to be fulfilled. Prayer is *attuning* yourself to the life of the world, to love, the force that moves the sun and the moon and the stars. — *Music of Silence*, xix

If it is true, as Bill Plotkin writes in his 2003 book Soulcraft, *that "there is a great longing within each of us" — both "the yearning for individual personal meaning, a way to contribute to life," along with a desire "to experience our oneness with the universe, with all of creation" — what Brother David has to say about prayer offers a direct response to that longing. Born from years of experience and his own scrupulous honesty, his "testing of the spirits," as it were, invites us to change our lives.*

But "to change our lives" is by no means grim or threatening. Brother David's writings on prayer bubble with both joy and wonder, while requiring "that condition of complete simplicity costing not less than everything," as T. S. Eliot puts it. At the same time, we hear the words of the mathematical cosmologist Brian Swimme, who raises the eye-widening possibility "that we are in the very middle of a fundamental change of course, something that takes place only once or twice every thousand years."

Thomas Berry, a self-styled geologian, historian of cultures, and coauthor with Brian Swimme of The Universe Story, *adds his own view, "that we live immersed in a sea of energy beyond all comprehension, and that it is ours, not by domination, but by invocation."*

PRAYERS AND PRAYERFULNESS

But where shall we start? I can only suggest that we start where we are, that we begin with what comes easiest. Why not start by surveying a typical day? What is it you tend to tackle with spontaneous mindfulness, so that without an effort your whole heart is in it? Maybe it's that first cup of coffee in the morning, the way it warms you and wakes you up, or taking your dog for a walk, or giving a little child a piggyback ride. Your heart is in it, and so you find meaning in it — not a meaning you could spell out in words, but a meaning in which you can rest. These are moments of intense prayerfulness, though we might never have thought of them as prayer. They show us the close connection between praying and playing. These moments when our heart finds ever so briefly rest in God are samples that give us a taste of what prayer is meant to be. If we could maintain this inner attitude, our whole life would become prayer.

— GHP, 47

Suppose, for example, you are reciting Psalms. If all goes well, this may be a truly prayerful experience. But all doesn't always go well. While reciting Psalms, you might experience nothing but a struggle against distractions. Half an hour later you are watering your African violets. Now, suddenly, the prayerfulness that never came during the prayers overwhelms you. You come alive from within. Your heart expands and embraces those velvet leaves, those blossoms looking up to you. The watering and drinking become a give-and-take so intimate that you cannot separate your pouring of the water from the roots' receiving, the flower's giving of joy from your drinking it in. And in a rush of gratefulness your heart celebrates this belonging together. As long as this lasts, everything has meaning, everything makes sense. You are communicating with your full self, with all there is, with God. Which was the real prayer, the Psalms or the watering of your African violets?   — *GHP,* 40

What matters is prayer, not prayers. But if this is so, if prayerfulness is all that counts, who needs prayers? The answer is simple: everyone. Prayers fill a need we all experience, the need to express our prayerfulness. We cannot be mindful without being grateful. As soon as we awake from taking everything for granted, there is at least a glimmer of surprise and a beginning of gratitude. But gratitude needs to express itself. We know the awkward feeling we get from an anonymous gift. When I receive one, it is as if something were bottled up within me, and all morning I find myself expressing something like thanks to everyone I meet, just to satisfy my own need for doing so. But something else happens. As I express my gratitude, I become more deeply aware of it. And the greater my awareness, the greater my need to express it. What happens here is a spiraling ascent, a process of growth in ever expanding circles around a steady center, a movement leading ever more deeply into gratefulness.

And so with prayers. As the expression of our prayerfulness, prayers make us more prayerful...   — *GHP,* 48–49

We can never learn prayerfulness by mere imitation from the outside.   —*GHP*, 84

Traditionally, prayer has been understood as the lifting of heart and mind to God. Anything that lifts our heart is prayer, though the moment may be too brief to actually say a "prayer" at the time.   —Brother David from "Man Alive" interview,
date unknown

The heart is where we meet God. But meeting God is prayer. So the heart is the meeting place with God in prayer.   —*GHP*, 31

In prayer, the heart drinks from the fountain of meaning.
—*GHP*, 37

Much of our life may be a wandering in the desert lands, but we do find springs of water. If what is called "God" means in the language of experience the ultimate Source of Meaning, then those moments that quench the thirst of the heart are moments of prayer.   —*GHP*, 39

In an interview with Kate Olson of the Fetzer Institute, Brother David, having talked about the way of love and emergent possibilities, goes on to say:

Where it's at for me is the God image in all the traditions is either warped or no longer acceptable for many people. I think my greatest interest is in the coming God image, in the evolving God image. And . . . the great question is, will the spiritual traditions rise, will they, as they are, as such, pass the threshold over which humanity is passing now in this axial age—and will they discover within themselves the God image that will carry us further in our development? It's inevitably coming. It's absolutely inevitably coming.

The question is not whether the spiritual traditions will give it to us. It comes from somewhere else. It comes from that depth that has given us these traditions in the first place. And so the question is which of the spiritual traditions will be wide enough to accept it, embrace it, celebrate it...live with it and pass it on? That's the great question.

— Originally located at *www.fetzer.org*
under Publications and Resources

A WHIMSICAL STORY

The food chain is a closed circle. On the biological level we humans are but one link in that chain. Wisdom will taste life and death with full awareness and will relish their tart intermingling. But wisdom has a wider perspective. Wisdom can see a food chain, as it were, that transcends biological life — not a closed circle, but an ever-rising helix. Father George Kosicki tells a delightfully whimsical story about this: Once upon a time, there was a dandelion growing in a meadow. The dandelion whispered to the amino acids and all the other nutrients in the soil, "How would you like to become dandelion? You need only to allow yourselves to be dissolved in a drop of water and I will suck you up through my roots. You won't feel a thing. But afterward, you will be able to grow and to flower and to fly away in the wind as a thousand miniature parachutes carrying seed." "Okay," said the amino acids and other nutrients in the soil. They let themselves be dissolved in rainwater and sucked up through the roots and they became dandelion.

The next morning, a rabbit came hopping across the meadow. "Good morning!" said the rabbit to the dandelion. "How would you like to become rabbit? You will have to allow yourself to be nibbled and chewed and swallowed. It hurts a little, but afterward you will be able to jump and bounce and romp in the moonlight, wiggle your ears, and have lots of baby rabbits." The dandelion was not overly enthusiastic, but the idea of hopping around sounded like a lot more fun than being stuck in one place. "Okay," said the dandelion with a sigh. It allowed itself to be munched and became rabbit.

Toward evening a hunter came by. "Good evening!" said the hunter to the rabbit (for it was an unusually polite hunter). "How would you like to become human? You must allow yourself to be shot dead, skinned, cooked in a stew, and eaten. This is not pleasant, I admit, but imagine, afterward you will be able to play yo-yo, sing in the shower, and fly in a jet plane." The rabbit was scared, but flying in a jet plane seemed so exciting; the idea was irresistible. Sniffling a little and wiping away a tear, the rabbit mumbled, "O.K.," went through with that ordeal, and became human.

But then, God came along. "Hi," God said. "How would you like to become...?"   —LH, 80–81

I remember when Tetsugen Glassman Roshi was being ordained the abbot of Riverside Zendo in New York. It was a grand affair. Zen teachers from all over the country were gathered together to celebrate the event, with candles and incense and white chrysanthemums and black and gold brocade garments. In the middle of this solemn celebration, the beeper on somebody's wristwatch suddenly went off. Everybody was sur-reptitiously looking around to find the poor guy to whom this had happened, because generally you are not even supposed to wear a wristwatch in the Zendo. To everybody's surprise, the new abbot himself interrupted the ceremony and said, "This was my wristwatch, and it was not a mistake. I have made a vow that regardless of what I am doing, I will interrupt it at noon and will think thoughts of peace." And then he invited everyone there to think thoughts of peace for a world that needs it.

That incident reminded me that the Angelus bells were really instituted in the first place to announce a prayer for peace. The bells ring when the day has reached its peak, at high noon. They were the bells for Sext in the monastery, but they invited every-one in the village to pray for peace. Wherever people were, in the fields or at their labors, in their shops or at home, when they heard the Angelus bells they would stop work and pray. Now all over the world, people are praying at high noon for peace, as we have done in the monastery for hundreds of years. How beautiful it would be to hear bells and gongs from famous shrines ring out peace on radio and television at high noon.

— *MS,* 71–72

Inseparable from Sext in the monastery is the practice of serving one another at mealtime. There are always servers at table who bring the food, and the monks themselves are encouraged by the rule of St. Benedict not to ask for anything they need, but always to look out for what a neighbor needs. (There's a famous story of a monk who notices as he is eating his soup that a mouse has dropped into his bowl. What is he to do? He is to pay attention to his neighbor's needs, not his own. So he helps

himself by calling the server and pointing out, "My neighbor
hasn't got a mouse.")   — *MS*, 73

THE JESUS PRAYER

*In February 1992, Richard Smoley interviewed Brother David
in an article entitled "Heroic Virtue" for* Gnosis Magazine.

Smoley: Where in Latin Christianity can somebody go for
contemplative practice?

Brother David: Well, my own practice is the Jesus Prayer, which
was originally Eastern but is widespread in Western Christianity also. First let me say that any practice — not only Christian
practices but other practices that are helpful for the spiritual
life — is to be encouraged. We don't look where it comes from.
I think St. Irenaeus said, "If some statement is true, don't ask
where it comes from. It's always the Holy Spirit." You can
apply this here too. You can say that if a practice is truly helpful, don't look where it comes from; it's always the Holy Spirit
that has inspired it.

But since you ask what is typically Western, I would mention
an unfortunately not well-known practice; it is typically Benedictine, St. Benedict mentions it, and it is called *lectio divina* —
"spiritual reading." It consists of reading, as the name says —
not necessarily, but typically — sacred scripture, but reading not
as much as you can but as little as you can. So you read only
one word, maybe, of a passage, and that already sends you,
because you give yourself completely to that. You let it speak
to you and it takes you where it comes from. So if one word

is enough, fine; if you need two words, all right; maybe you need a whole sentence, all right; maybe you need a whole page or two, and that's all right still, but the less the better. And then this reading sends you into — I would not say reflecting on what you have read, because that is too active — but into basking in it, savoring it, and that usually lasts for a little while, depending on your psychological state. Sooner or later you begin to daydream, and then you can come back to the next word or the next sentence or the next page, so that the reading is really like a landing strip from which to take off, and whenever you can't stay in the air anymore, you come back down to it, taxi, and take off again. *Lectio divina* is a practice that has been continuously in use in the Benedictine tradition for fifteen hundred years. There are now many lay people who practice it too, and they find it very helpful. But it isn't as well known as it should be. And it is a typical Western meditation practice.

Smoley: Perhaps you'd like to say a little bit about your own practice with the Jesus Prayer. I'm not familiar with those beads you're holding, for example.

Brother David: Well, I made them. I wear them on my finger as a ring. They have ten beads, so I can use them as a rosary. The moving of the beads sets in motion a psychomotor circular process. It takes some practice, but every time you move the bead, it lets this prayer run off on a subliminal level. While I talk with you or do other things, moving the beads triggers something within me that lets this prayer flash through my heart.

As you know, there are many different forms of the Jesus Prayer, longer and shorter forms. I really use only the short form: "Lord Jesus, mercy; Lord Jesus, mercy." I find the others too long; I get distracted. Also with my breathing, "Lord Jesus, mercy; Lord Jesus, mercy" works better. Besides, I think there is a lot of emphasis in our tradition on sins, and the longer form, "Have mercy on me, a sinner" reinforces that emphasis.

We certainly are sinners, rightly understood. Not even so much personally. But we live in a world of alienation, of sin; no matter how good-willed you are, you really can't help causing millions of people in the Third World to be exploited, just by the fact that you live in the First World. This is sin, much more than your little peccadilloes. I really am quite aware of this sinfulness. But I don't think it is necessary to rub it in with every breath. I'd rather praise God for having forgiven and overcome sin. When I say, "Lord Jesus, mercy," that can be a call for mercy, but most of the time it means, "What mercy you are showing!" It's a prayer of praise and thanksgiving.

— "Heroic Virtue"

BEAUTY

While beauty is not in itself prayer, it certainly can call forth prayerfulness. In the following passage, we see how attitudes are changed by beauty acting on our awareness. John O'Donohue expresses his prayer for us all so beautifully: "May you experience each day as a sacred gift woven around the heart of wonder."

Beauty transforms the beholder. Beauty is winning. It wins you over. Even goodness and truth will not be fully convincing to the human heart unless they are gifted with a gracefulness and ease that makes them beautiful. Take any period in history. Who is still convinced by the arguments of its politicians, its philosophers, even its theologians? But think of the poets of the same period or listen to its music. We take a dim view of the hopes that inspired the crusaders. But their hope inspired the cathedrals and still shines from every arch, sill, and coping stone. Beauty, even in its most limited realization, holds an unquestionable promise of illimitable fulfillment. When we contemplate, say, the great rose window at Chartres, we simply know what it means that "we rejoice in hope of the glory of God" (Rom. 5:2).

Beauty is useless, superfluous, like all great things in life. Is not the universe itself a totally superfluous firework of divine glory, and *therefore* so priceless? Useful things have a price. But who can assess the value of a poem in dollars and cents? Who can put a price tag on a kiss? ... When Jesus says, "Behold the lilies" (Matt. 6:28), he is inviting each one of us to take beauty seriously in all its uselessness. What will this mean for our daily life?   *— GHP*, 154–55

We might think of prayers as the poetry of our prayer life. A poem celebrates life and in that celebration becomes itself a high point of life. We look with the eyes of our heart, are overawed by the wonders we see, and celebrate that vision by a gesture that taps the very source of life. But it can be said much more simply: Prayer is grateful living.   *— GHP*, 59

WHERE ANGELS DWELL

"It is not known precisely where angels dwell," Voltaire wrote, tongue in cheek. Their lack of a precise address made him wonder if they existed at all. Today, a more enlightened view about angels is gaining ground, thanks to the very Age of Enlightenment that Voltaire spearheaded.

Gratefully freed from taking metaphor literally, our age is no longer concerned with the wingspan of angels, their sex, or the question of how many of them can dance on the head of a pin. Instead, we focus on the meaning of their name: *angel* originally meant *mounted courier* or *messenger.*

Angels as messengers are alive and well today, and we get along without knowing precisely where they dwell. What matters is that they pop up where we least expect them. We meet an angel whenever a life-giving message touches a human heart. We may feel an angel's caress in the touch of a human hand, or meet an angel's gaze as we look into the eyes of a dog or a cat. Angels have even been known to jump out from behind bushes and go "Boo!" as children who hide to scare us a little and then squeeze us a tight hug. The only thing we know for sure about angels is that they are unpredictable — like everything else that is truly alive.

The angels who inspired these pages (*Music of Silence,* 1998, 2002) have made many friends since this book first appeared — so many that there is need for a new edition.

It has given me great joy to receive messages from readers who thank me for introducing them to angels they never knew to be around. They tell me that hours of their days and nights have turned into couriers for them each with a distinctive dispatch. They share their delight at learning to attune the ears of their hearts to the heavenly hosts announcing with myriad tongues the gracious message of each hour, each unmistakably different. They even tell me that they hear music now, angelic music where they used to hear merely clocks ticking.

There is a bond now between my readers and me. We have become friends through the angelic friends we share. It feels good to walk in their company. Together now with others whom I have never seen, I rise each morning to meet a procession of bearers of good tiding — good, even when they are difficult; good, because uplifting whenever I rise to the occasion; good, because shared.

When I encounter in the great night silence before dawn the maker of music which only the heart can hear, I know that I am not alone. When I join the proclaimer of new light in raising my eyes to still-hidden blessings, I know that others out there open their hearts with me in trust and in hope. Together we ready ourselves for creative action when we hear the green drummer beat the drum at the door of another day of work. Together we dance in the Spirit when the angel of the third hour raises the fiddle — after all, who would want to dance alone? The trumpet blast of high noon makes not only my own heart tremble; I know that other hearts out there reverberate with this sound. Together our hearts quiet down in response to the angel who muffles the sound of the tambourine, as day declines and evening shadows rise. Our hearts are joined as we gaze at the angel of the evening star, as we close our eyes in the company of the final angel, under whose heavy eyelids dreams ripen to sweetness.

All these encounters with angels take place not in otherworldly seclusion, but amid the buzz of daily business at its busiest. This is the best part of it. This is good news. We do not have to get out of the stream of daily life; its undertows and eddies have no power to drown us. We need only look through the rushing waters to the stillness in its depth. This takes some practice, but it can be done. We can do it in the midst of rush-hour traffic or while waiting in the check-out line at the supermarket. In an elevator or at the Laundromat we can take a few seconds to readjust our inner gaze to greater depth. We can do this even in front of our computer screen.

A team of wingless angels has set up an interactive website (*www.gratefulness.org*) that allows us to meet the angels of each sacred hour on the Internet. Serene images. One deep look at them will clear our vision, but we may want to keep gazing. Meanwhile we can listen to the Latin hymn for the particular hour at which we are meditating: monastic chanting, angel music. We may not know precisely where else angels dwell, but one thing is certain (and how could Voltaire have suspected it?): angels dwell even in cyberspace.

May all those who peruse this book — with or without its website support — meet angels everywhere and at every hour. This is my heartfelt wish for its new launching.

— Preface to *MS,* xxi–xxiv

Prayer is unlimited mindfulness. And this coincides with the most traditional notion of prayer while it broadens the concept immensely. For you have always known that you can "say your prayers" without really having prayed. And when we ask: "What is it, then, that makes prayers, prayer?" The answer is "recollection." (Mindfulness means the same and is a term less worn by use and abuse.) If you say your prayers mindfully, you really pray. Well then, what really matters is obviously mindfulness, recollection, openness. The gesture of the open hands, raised in prayer, is in typical contrast to the clenched fist that tries to hold on to things. Prayerful recollection is loving openness to receive the meaning conveyed by a given moment. Set times for prayer are certainly necessary to cultivate prayerfulness, but should we restrict prayer to set times? If we know what it means to say prayers mindfully, we ought to be able to do everything with the same mindfulness. And thus everything becomes prayer; everything becomes celebration. Everything becomes celebration as we learn to take things one by one, moment by moment; to single everything out for grateful consideration. —*LH*, 109–10

4

Time —
The Perfection of the Moment

> At any moment the fully present mind can shatter time and
> burst into Now. — *LH*, 109

*Brother David has experience of time both in the monastery,
during periods of living as a hermit, and out on the road, on
his many extensive lecture tours that traverse all five continents.
To give but one example, on a lecture tour in Australia, he gave
140 lectures and traveled 12,000 miles within Australia without back-tracking. And then, of course, he has conversations
with countless friends as he travels. Yet time for him is different
than it is for most of us, unconsciously caught as we are in a
feverish round of "getting things done," ticking things off our
lists. It doesn't require much reading of what Brother David
has written to realize that the "great fullness" he writes about
is not that — it is about living according to the real rhythms
of the day: to live with awareness of the coming of the light
as we struggle to hit the day; of the magic of high noon, when
the Angelus used to ring out from every village church across
Europe; to the moment we finally lay our heads on the pillow.*

That is, if we are blessed to have shelter that is warm and dry and reasonably quiet. Brother David is always conscious of the millions who do not know these blessings. He writes about time in a way that may turn our worlds upside down.

Saturated with information but often bereft of meaning, we feel caught in a never-ending swirl of duties and demands, things to finish, things to put right. Yet as we dart anxiously from one activity to the next, we sense that there is more to life than our worldly agendas.

Our uneasiness and our frantic scrambling are caused by our distorted sense of time, which seems to be continually running out. Western culture reinforces this misconception of time as a limited commodity. We are always meeting *dead*lines; we are always short on time; we are always running out of time.

Chant music evokes a different relationship to time, which while precious, is not scarce. It conjures the archetype of the monk's way of life, wherein time flows harmoniously; the time available is in proportion to the task at hand. The pure, serene, yet soaring sounds of the chant remind us that there *is* another way to live in this noisy, distracted world, and this way is not as out of reach as it might seem.

When listening to Gregorian chant, we become aware not only of the blended voices of the monks, but also of an almost inaudible echo, an additional dimension of depth to the music. It is the sacred, transcendental quality of the melodic lines, chanted in a high-ceilinged oratory, that many find so appealing about Gregorian chant. And it is this depth dimension that is so much like the *now* dimension of time. For now does not occur in chronological time, but transcends it. Here time is not conceived as running out, but as rising like water in a well, rising to that fullness of time that is now.   — *MS*, 1

ABOUT THE "HOURS"

What is an "hour"? Is it nothing more than a unit of time composed of sixty minutes? Is it measured by numbers or by impressions, feelings, moods? Like the seasons of the year, the seasons of the day differ by the way we experience them. Each hour we encounter has a character and a presence infinitely richer and more complex than clock time. As Brother David puts it, "As a messenger from another dimension — an angel as it were — an hour has its own unique significance." As monasticism spread, the practice of specified hours and liturgical formats began to develop and become standardized to mark times of the day such as the Coming of the Light, High Noon, When Darkness Comes, to mention but a few. Around the year 484, St. Sabbas began the process of recording the liturgical practices around Jerusalem. In 525, St. Benedict of Nursia wrote the first official Western manual for praying the Hours. Different traditions may have different names or times of the day when people gather to pray, celebrating "the liturgy of the hours."

The monastic understanding of the word "hour" goes back to a Greek word, *hora*, which is older than our notion of a day broken up into twenty-four-hour segments. The original notion of hour is something quite different from a unit of time composed of sixty minutes. It is not a numerical measure; it is a soul measure.

We come closer to an appreciation of the original meaning of hour when we reflect on the seasons of the year. They betoken the original understanding, in which a season is a mood and an experience, not an exact period that starts, say, on the twenty-first of December and ends on the twenty-first of March. In fact, we're usually surprised when we find in the calendar that the first day of winter is the twenty-first of December, because either winter has long been here, or it's not yet winter at all. It's rare that any season really starts on its assigned date. Rather, seasons are qualitative experiences: We sense a subtle difference in the quality of light, the length of daylight, the feel of the air on our skin. We know intuitively that something is happening in nature.   — *MS,* 2–3

In one of his own poems, Brother David gives expression to this further dimension, this other measure of time, as he gathers the gifts of the seasons, rounding out the year, clothing it in color and rhythm in the following paean of grateful praise:

Thanksgiving Song

As the Great Dynamo who powers the wheels of seasons
    and years
Turns autumn once more into winter,
At this season of Thanksgiving,
We give thanks for all seasons.

For winter, who strips trees to their basic design,
For stark, minimalist winter,
We give thanks.
May we let go, and grow bright as stars in a clear, frosty
    night,

The more we are stripped of what we thought we could
    not do without.

For the springtime that bursts forth,
Just when we think winter will never end,
For irrepressible springtime
We give thanks.
May we never forget the crippled, wind-beaten trees,
How they, too, bud, green and bloom,
May we, too, take courage to bloom where we are
    planted.

For summer, when fruit begins to ripen more and more,
For the green, swelling high tide of summer
We give thanks.
May we trust that time is not running out, but coming to
    fulfillment,
May we wait patiently while time ripens.

For autumn and its slow growing fruition
For that season of ultimate rise and fall
We give thanks.
May we gracefully rise to the occasion of our own falling,
Giving ourselves just enough time to go beyond time
To the great Now
At the quiet center of the turning wheels.

We give thanks for all seasons
At this season of Thanksgiving.

The hours are the seasons of the day, and they were originally understood in a mythical way. Earlier generations of our

human race, not ruled by alarm clocks, saw the hours personi-
fied, encountered them as messengers of eternity in the natural
flow of time growing, blossoming, bearing fruit. In the unfolding rhythm of everything that grows and changes on earth each
hour had a character and presence infinitely richer and more
complex than our sterile clock time. As messenger from another
dimension — an angel as it were — each hour was understood
to have its own significance.

Today, even in our busy city schedules, we notice that pre-
dawn, early morning, midmorning, and high noon each have
qualities all their own. Midafternoon, the time the shadows
lengthen, has a different character from the time when it gets
dark and we turn on the lights.

A canonical hour thus is more a presence than a measure-
ment. The hours that call the monks together for prayer and
chant are angels we encounter at different points in the day.
The hours are called canonical, since the word "canon" originally meant a measuring rod, and it is by its different moods
that the day is measured. But "canon" can also mean a trellis,
like a lattice that supports vines. So we can also think of the
canonical hours as the frame by which the monastic day, indeed
the monastic life, is supported.

The hours are the inner structure for living consciously and
responsively through the stages of the day. The monastic relationship to time through the canonical hours sensitizes us to
the nuances of time. And as this sensitivity deepens, we become
more available to the present moment.

The responsive singing of chant in each hour helps monks to
find the elusive now dimension of our lives. Chant primes us to
respond to the call of each hour, for real living happens not in
clock time, not in chronological time (from the Greek *chronos*)

but in what the Greeks called the *kairos,* time as opportunity
or encounter. From the monastic perspective, time is a series of
opportunities, of encounters. We live in the now by attuning
ourselves to the calls of each moment, listening and responding
to what each hour, each situation, brings.   — *MS, 3–5*

The message of the [monastic] hours is to live daily with the *real*
rhythms of the day. To live responsively, consciously, and inten-
tionally directing our lives from within, not being swept along
by the demands of the clock, by external agendas, by mere
reactions to whatever happens. By living in the real rhythms,
we ourselves become more real. We learn to listen to the music
of this moment, to hear its sweet implorings, its sober directives.
We learn to dance a little in our hearts, to open our inner gates
a crack more, to hearken to the music of silence, the divine life
breath of the universe.   — *MS,* 116

To the here, the holy ground, belongs the now, the Kairos, the
holy moment, the acceptable time, the today of which we sing
in the liturgy over and over again. "Today, when you hear his
voice, harden not your hearts" — a decisive passage. And this
today is always.   — *LH,* 14

There are occasions when it is time for something, whether you
like it or not. And if you come only five minutes late, the sun is
not going to re-rise for you; it is not going to re-set for you; and
noon is not going to come a little later because you turned the
clock back.   — *LH,* 15

If we envision time as a line that leads from the future into the
past, then the past is continuously eating up the future without

the least remnant. As long as we think of "now" as a very short stretch of time, nothing prevents us from cutting that stretch in half, and half again. Because chronological time can always be further subdivided, there is no "now" on our clocks, no "still center" to be found in clock time. To think of time in this way is not just to play with words; it's a mental experiment we can do to bring home to ourselves that, in knowing what now means, we are experiencing something that transcends time: eternity.

Eternity is not a long, long time. Eternity is the opposite of time: it is no time. It is, as Augustine said, "The now that does not pass away." We cannot reach that now by proceeding in mere chronological sequence, yet it is accessible at any moment as the mysterious fullness of time.

We are welcomed into time's mystery once in a while in our most alive moments, in our peak experiences. We say of those moments, "Time seemed to stand still," or "So much was crammed into one little moment," or "Hours passed and it seemed like just a flash, a second." Our sense of time is altered in those moments of deep and intense experience, so we know what that means. We feel at home in that now, in that eternity, because that is the only place where we really *are*. We cannot *be* in the future and we cannot *be* in the past; we can only *be* in the present. We are only real to the extent to which we are living in the present here and now.   — *MS*, 7–8

The monks rise and go to sleep, work and celebrate, when "it is time." They are only "keeping" the time, not "setting" it. At the first sound of the bell, the monk is to let loose whatever he is engaged in, and turn to that for which it is time. What matters is the letting loose. It is liberation. Through it the time which was "not our time," becomes ours because we give ourselves to it. Swinging with the living seasons you are "in tune with the world," and it is all yours.   — *LH*, 103–4

Long before the official expiration date of our life expectancy, we begin to notice a gradual diminishment of sensual keenness. If we don't want to get stuck in dead-end living we need to push through to "life-end" dying. The sooner we start, the better. Active dying is life-affirming. Its secret of success: letting go. This gives us great inner freedom; freedom to ask: what is it time for now? Time to find what we have always been after, the joy at the core of pleasure, the joy that outlasts pleasure.
                                                              — *LH*, 54

LEISURE

Brother David sees leisure not as a privilege, but as a virtue. He writes about the magnificent superfluities of life.

Leisure is the expression of detachment with regard to time. For the leisure of monks is not the privilege of those who can afford to take time; it is the virtue of those who give to everything they do the time it deserves to take.

Within the monastery the listening which is the essence of this spiritual discipline expresses itself in bringing life into harmony with the cosmic rhythm of seasons and hours, with "time, not our time" as T. S. Eliot calls it...the moment in which we truly listen is "a moment in and out of time."

...Listen to the soundless bell of "time, not our time," wherever it be and the doing of whatever needs to be done when it is time— "now, and at the hour of our death."   — *LH*, 5

We learn to live fully in the measure in which we learn to live leisurely. Leisure is a virtue, not a luxury. Leisure is the virtue of those who take their time in order to give to each task as much time as it deserves to take. — *GHP*, 206

To recover a healthy understanding of leisure is to come a long way toward understanding contemplation. But few words we use are as misunderstood as the word "leisure." This shows itself right away when we speak of work and leisure as a pair of opposites. Are the two poles of activity really work and leisure? If this were so, how could we speak of leisurely work? It would be a blatant contradiction. We know, however, that working leisurely is no contradiction at all. In fact, work ought to be done with leisure, if it is to be done well.

What then is the opposite of work? It is play. These are the two poles of all activity: work and play. And what we have come to understand about purpose and meaning will help us see this more clearly. Whenever you work, you work for some purpose. If it weren't for that purpose, you'd have better things to do than work. Work and purpose are so closely connected that your work comes to an end, once your purpose is achieved. Or how are you going to continue fixing your car once it is fixed?...

In play, all the emphasis falls on the meaning of your activity. ...Play needs no purpose. That is why play can go on and on as long as players find it meaningful. After all, we do not dance in order to get somewhere. We dance around and around. A piece of music doesn't come to an end when its purpose is accomplished. It has no purpose, strictly speaking. It is the playful unfolding of a meaning that is there in each of its movements, in every theme, every passage: a celebration of meaning. Pachel-bel's Canon is one of the magnificent superfluities of life. Every time I listen to it, I realize anew that some of the most super-fluous things are the most important for us because they give meaning to our human life.

We need this kind of experience to correct our worldview. Too easily are we inclined to imagine that God created this world for a purpose. We are so caught up in purpose that we would feel more comfortable if God shared our preoccupation with work. But God plays. The birds in a single tree are suffi-cient proof that God did not set out with a divine no-nonsense attitude to make a creature that would perfectly achieve the pur-pose of a bird. What could that purpose be? I wonder. There are titmice, juncos, and chickadees; woodpeckers, gold finches, starlings, and crows. The only bird God never created is the no-nonsense bird. As we open our eyes and hearts to God's cre-ation, we quickly perceive that God is a playful God, a God of leisure. . . .

When our purposeful work also is meaningful, we will have a good time in the midst of it. Then we will not be so eager to get it over with. If you spend only minutes a day getting this or that over with, you may be squandering days, weeks, years in the course of a lifetime. Meaningless work is a form of killing time. But leisure makes time come alive. The Chinese character for being busy is also made up of two elements: heart and killing. A timely warning. Our very heartbeat is healthy only when it is leisurely.

The heart is a leisurely muscle. It differs from all other mus-cles. How many push-ups can you make before the muscles in your arms and stomach get so tired that you have to stop? But your heart muscle goes on working for as long as you live. It does not get tired, because there is a phase of rest built into every single heartbeat. Our physical heart works leisurely. And when we speak of the heart in a wider sense, the idea that life-giving leisure lies at the very center is implied. Never to lose sight of that central place of leisure in our life would keep us youthful. — *GHP*, 71–75

HAIKU

Haiku poetry, which Brother David has described as an inexhaustible topic, encapsulates time into what Patricia Donegan, author of Haiku Mind, *calls "a crystalline moment of heightened awareness, . . . a deep reminder for us to pause and to be present to the details of the everyday." As Brother David has said, to discover the haiku, to enter more deeply into it, to revel in its delights would be worthwhile in itself. But there is more . . .*

A haiku does not talk about an experience: a haiku triggers an experience — your own. — *LH*, 88

The haiku is, paradoxically, a poem about silence. Its very core is silence. There is probably no shorter poetic form in world literature than the classical haiku with its seventeen syllables, and yet the masters put these seventeen syllables down with a gesture of apology, which makes it clear that words merely serve the silence. All that matters is the silence. The haiku is a scaffold of words; what is being constructed is a poem of silence; and when it is ready, the poet gives a little kick, as it were, to the scaffold. It tumbles, and silence alone stands.

Evening rain
The banana leaf
Speaks of it first

We can almost hear the first big raindrops falling one by one. But this is already the moment after the decisive one; the moment after the one that held its breath in limitless anticipation. This is not a poem about rain, but about the silence before the rain. A strange poem, the haiku! It zeroes in on the here and now which is nowhere. It celebrates the all-oneness of aloneness in all the bliss of its poignant pain. It stakes out territory for the discovery precisely where life is most daily. And while setting up landmarks of adventure, it wipes out its own footprints. It denies itself. For it shoots words like arrows at the target of silence. Every word that hits the mark returns to the silence out of which it came.

Does this sound paradoxical? It certainly is, yet, no more paradoxical than you are to yourself. For the haiku merely mirrors the paradox of the "still point" — the paradox of the human heart. In a masterly haiku what it means to be human has been crystallized. Crystallized, not petrified. Not like rock, but lightly as in a snowflake that will melt and become a drop of water as soon as it touches you. Crystallized in the haiku, the paradox is not dispelled. It is brought home; it is made bearable; you can stand under it and rejoice in it as children rejoice in snowflakes. And thus, standing for once under the paradox rather than over against it, you can understand; you can understand yourself.

Self-understanding attained at the "still point"; this is the core of the Peak Experience; the burden of T. S. Eliot's *Four Quartets;* the hidden source of haiku poetry; the goal of the monk. Of course the goal is the same for all of us, and monastic life is but one possible way of attaining this goal...in a measure, it can be understood by every human being.

> ...the moment in and out of time,
> The distraction fit, lost in a shaft of sunlight,
> The wild thyme unseen, or the winter lightning
> Or the waterfall, or music heard so deeply
> That it is not heard at all, but you are the music
> While the music lasts.

...If you have seen in a flash that everything makes sense as soon as you go beyond reasoning, you will be ready to understand why some men and women should devote their whole life to the pursuit of this paradox.　　　　 — *LH*, 96–97, 98, 99

MONASTIC AWARENESS

Monastic training is unhurried and down to earth: sweeping, cooking, washing; serving at table or at the altar; reading books or filing library cards; digging, typing, haying, plumbing — but all of this with that affectionate detachment which makes the place where you are the navel of the universe.

To this monastic awareness of place belongs a distinctively monastic awareness of time.

> The time of the seasons and the constellations
> The time of milking and the time of harvest...[1]

---

1. T. S. Eliot, *Four Quartets, East Coker,* I:421.

The time of "the seabell's perpetual angelus" on the coast where

> The tolling bell
> Measures time not our time, rung by the unhurried
> Ground swell, a time
> Older than the time of chronometers, older
> Than time counted ... [2]

And the "unhurried ground swell" becomes an image of that "love expanding beyond desire," detached but not indifferent, on the contrary, alert and responsible — for the time measured by the tolling bell is "not our time." We are called. We must respond....

The angelus bell and the gong, the clapper, the drum, the sounding board are so many ways of keeping time "not our time."

...This detachment from time and place through which everything becomes ours because we are fully present in the here and now, this is the seed fruit of monastic detachment, its ultimate accomplishment containing in seed everything....

All other renunciation is included in the monk's affectionate detachment from the here and now. It points to that ultimate self-detachment in which our true Self is found.... Detachment, understood in this truly catholic, i.e., all-embracing sense, leads us directly to monastic celibacy, because....

Celibacy certainly belongs in the context of "expanding of love beyond desire, and so, liberation."[3] Seen in this light, the accent switches from the aspect of dispossession, deprivation, renunciation to the aspect of expansion, liberation, fulfillment.

2. T. S. Eliot, *The Dry Salvages,* I:34–39.
3. T. S. Eliot, *Four Quartets, Little Gidding,* III:157f.

In the context of the Peak Experience it makes sense to say that the monk is a celibate, a loner, because his oneness with all is expanding beyond desire. And it is equally true to say that he can embrace this oneness with all only because (and in so far as) he is truly alone. Celibacy is the daring attempt to sustain the "condition of extreme simplicity" in which solitude and togetherness merge so that aloneness becomes all-oneness.

This experience of concord with oneself and with all, a concord realized at the heart of the universe, at the still point — this experience is always granted gratis. But it is one thing to be surprised by it in a flash in the "moment of happiness... the sudden illumination" and quite a different thing to sustain a life centered on this still point, to remain "still and still moving." For this we need the support of others embarked on the same venture. (Even the hermit needs this support, though less tangibly.) Monastic solitude must be supported by togetherness.

It is surprising how much togetherness one needs in order to save aloneness from deteriorating into loneliness. Here lies the root of monastic community. Solitude and togetherness make each other possible. Take away solitude, and togetherness becomes subhuman gregariousness; take away togetherness and solitude becomes desolation.

Community can exist only in the tension between solitude and togetherness. The delicate balance between solitude and togetherness will determine what kind of community it shall be. In the togetherness community of which married life is the prototype, togetherness is the measure of solitude: each of the partners must have as much solitude as they need for rich and full togetherness.   —*LH*, 102–6

THE ALL-ONENESS
OF ALONENESS

In the summer 1992 issue of Gnosis Magazine, *Richard Smoley interviewed Brother David. The interview was entitled "Heroic Virtue." After a more general discussion of asceticism:*

Brother David: Very few people talk about the asceticism of family life. At least from the perspective of a monk, the asceticism of family life is greater than that of the monastery. That is not something I have invented. St. Bernard of Clairvaux spoke about it already as long ago as the eleventh century: how monks should have the greatest respect for householders, because if they're serious about living their Christian faith, we have a lot to learn from them. There's a built-in asceticism in a householder's life that you can't avoid. Monks get up at night to pray, but if they decide not to do so, they don't get up. There's no built-in absolute necessity to do so. But if your baby cries in the middle of the night, you have to get up; there's no maybe about it.

And so with almost every one of the ascetic disciplines; in their own way, they're imposed on the householder.

Monks are aware of this, and not only in the Christian tradition. In the Buddhist tradition, the Sufi tradition, and the other traditions too.

Smoley: What about celibacy? What are the uses of celibacy? Is sexual energy transformed into something higher?

Brother David: I can only tell you about it from my point of view. I don't want to talk about things that I have not personally experienced. I know of people whom I very much respect who would give you a totally different interpretation of celibacy. Mother Tessa, for example, is a Carmelite monastic; she speaks beautifully about celibacy in terms of bridal symbolism. Carmelites inherited the imagery of the bride of Christ from St. Teresa and St. John of the Cross. It's beautiful and poetic, but it's a bit foreign to my personal experience.

I approach celibacy from a very practical point of view. I see sexuality as the bodily expression of our relatedness to others. It's present in every relationship, even the most casual, and we do well to make sure the expression is genuine. If monastics totally belong to everyone they meet — and that's their calling — how can they genuinely express this in the realm of sexuality? Total promiscuity might be one way, but that's not very practical. The most realistic form is that of relating to everybody as brother or sister — celibacy. The restrictions placed upon our sexuality are not imposed on celibates because there is something wrong with sexuality, but only because if you have set yourself certain goals in life, you have to fit the use of your sexuality to these goals. And the goals that monastics have set themselves — mindfulness, full belonging to all — these goals put very severe limits on the use of sexuality.

The real glory of celibacy comes not from having freed yourself from something that is inglorious; on the contrary, you let go of it with the greatest regret. The glory comes from having so single-mindedly set yourself on something that you're holding up — that quest for total mindfulness and universal belonging — that you're even willing to deprive yourself, and others possibly, of something so glorious as sexuality.

— "Heroic Virtue"

Monks in community help one another in love to cultivate and sustain genuine aloneness. No one can do without this support. Even solitary explorers must still rely on the team that stands behind them. The stakes of this exploration are high....

Supported "at the still point," we must explore the together dimension of solitude, the all-oneness of aloneness....

What monks are after is not "knowledge derived," but immediate knowledge; not the knowledge we can grasp, of which we can take hold, but the meaning that speaks to us in the experience, hits us, "grabs" us, takes hold of us. And just as we saw that "time, not our time" gives itself to us as soon as we let loose in detachment and give ourselves over to its liberating power, so the meaning for which we are searching in life gives itself to us as soon as we renounce the effort to grasp it and begin to listen to it. Knowledge tries to grasp; wisdom listens. Listening wisdom: that is obedience. Obviously, obedience here is taken in its most comprehensive sense. We must not restrict obedience to the notion of "doing someone else's will." ... Submission is not an end in itself. It is a means, and only one of various means. The end is obedience in its full sense as a loving listening to the meaning that comes to us through everything and every person and every situation.

—*LH*, 106–7

In time that grows old, hope sees time that is with child.

—*GHP*, 148

5

The Living Voice of Poetry

What is exile?...Exile is being used to something, taking it for granted. Wherever you are, if you take it for granted, you are in exile. It's your deadness that exiles you. And if you come alive! — wherever you are, you will recognize that you are on holy ground.　　　— "Enjoying Poetry"

It is clear that poetry feeds the wellsprings of Brother David's life and vitality. One has only to read any one of his books to find it laced with poetry. Rainer Maria Rilke and T. S. Eliot stand out as mentors in the unfolding of his life, but there are many others. One can sense him reveling in the language of Gerard Manley Hopkins.

Bill Moyers, in an interview recorded in his 1999 book, Fooling with Words — A Celebration of Poets and Their Craft *(90), refers to Jane Hirschfield as having once said that a good poem can set its listener adrift in a small raft under a vast night sky of stars. She also wrote, "We travel by poem" and said "One person's word-wakened knowledge becomes another's." As we reflect on how Brother David uses poems from many sources in all his teaching, we can see that poetry is his "word-wakened knowledge."*

Brother David takes a cue from Rilke's use of his poem "Archaic Torso of Apollo," in which Rilke makes his readers feel that they are gazing at the sculpture that he sets before them rather than describes. They are all eyes. But suddenly, Rilke turns the perspective right around and says: "There is no place that does not see you." He closes the poem abruptly with, "You must change your life."

Brother David uses poetry in the same way, challenging people as he shows them how to become more alive, to know themselves blessed and so to bless, and to drink deeply from life. Always in the context of grateful service — he shows us how poetry can magnify and clarify our experience of the world. As Australian poet Judith Wright puts it, "When poetry withers in us, the greater part of experience and reality wither too; and when this happens, we live in a desolate world of facts, not of truth — a world scarcely worth the trouble of living in."

Brother David sees this passage as a key insight. Even back in 1983 he understood that "the environmental abuses we perpetuate all over the world are largely the results of poetry starvation. It is not only that 'poetry takes the violence out of reason,' as J. F. Kennedy put it. Poetry gives us access to those reasons of the heart which reason cannot fathom. Only the poet within each of us has eyes for the inherent sacredness of nature."

What follows are some excerpts from a workshop given by Brother David in 1992 called "Enjoying Poetry":

AT THE STILL POINT
OF THE TURNING WORLD

There are moments in our lives that are *still points*. That means they are turning points in the movement of our lives, moments where the movement seems to stand still. In those moments our life comes together. As long as life remains dynamic and moves on, there is continuous change, one thing after the other. Then comes this turning point, as in a dance, where suddenly the whole dance seems to be contained in one particular point.

A good example might be Greek sculpture. In Greek sculpture you often have some dynamic motion depicted, like the famous Disk Thrower. But how do you cast a disk thrower into bronze — something that has stood there, unmoved, for two and a half thousand years, and that's supposed to be throwing a disk? How are you going to go about that? The whole skill of the artist, or a great aspect of the skill, consists of catching exactly that point when the movement of throwing this disk seems to stand perfectly still, and all that goes before and all that follows after is contained in this one movement. As you walk around the statue of the Disk Thrower, it seems to move and it seems to somehow throw this disk. At any rate, you have this quiet moment caught in sculpture.

Sometimes you also have that moment in dance, when after a very dynamic movement everything seems to come to a standstill. And that's really the high point — some pirouette or something like that. You can also sometimes see it in skating.

In our everyday lives, we have these moments where the movement of our activity — of a particular activity — seems to almost come to a standstill, but *not* because it slows down, but on the contrary because it goes so fast — like a flame that is really burning well will seem to be perfectly still. It flickers and moves before it burns perfectly; then it seems to stand still. I am talking about that kind of stillness — or the stillness of the hawk before it dives down — perfectly still, standing in the air. Or the famous example of a top that spins so fast that it seems to stand still.

Referring to a turning point, Rilke says, "That great Artist who creates all of life, or designs all of life, or the whole universe, is only really interested in this turning." Exactly as the Greek sculptor was only interested in catching that point where the movement seems to stand still. How can he say that? What he's expressing here is a truth that we are all very familiar with, namely, that at *this* moment we feel particularly in touch with the Source of that great design of life. Or the Designer, if you want to personalize it. In those moments, everything makes sense. What comes before seems to lead up to this moment, what comes after seems to grow from a seed contained in that moment. We can experience this. The poetic image that the Great Designer is only interested in that particular turning point expresses a profound human truth.

T. S. Eliot says, "Except for the point, the still point, there would be no dance." Except for that point, there would be no dance. There would just be your limbs flailing around. The dance comes about because there is this still point. He goes on to say, "and there is only the dance." Except for the point, the still point, there would be no dance. And there is *only* the dance.

This means that everything in life is just as Rilke says — *all* of life and the world, everything earthly, is part of this great design. T. S. Eliot calls it the Great Dance, which comes from the first of the *Four Quartets:*

At the still point of the turning world. Neither flesh nor
    fleshless;
Neither from nor towards; at the still point, there the
    dance is,
But neither arrest nor movement. And do not call it fixity,
Where past and future are gathered. Neither movement
    from nor towards,
Neither ascent nor decline.[1]

Then come those lines,

Except for the point, the still point,
There would be no dance, and there is only the dance.

At the still point of the turning world. In other words, we are
no longer talking about the particular still point moment in my
life, or your life, or in someone else's life. But about that still
point for the whole world, for the whole universe. How can we
do that? Because that turning point is the Now. In that moment
we know what Now is. It's not past, it's not was, it's not future.
When we are really present, we are delighted to experience these
turning points. Most of the time we are *not* present where we
are. Then for one moment we are really present. In another part
of the *Four Quartets* Eliot says, "And all is always Now."

I hope you have located this, even tentatively, in your own
experience. The Now, the still point of the turning world is the
turning point of which Rilke speaks. That is the point of poetry.
All poetry that is worth its salt is *always* in one way or another
about that turning point.

---

1. T. S. Eliot, *Four Quartets, Burnt Norton*, 11.

I use both terms "still point" and "turning point," which can be confusing. By "turning point" I do not mean a continuous movement of turning, turning, turning, but the point at which it turns, the point where as it turns it stands still. That's why Eliot puts these adjectives of extremes next to one another. "Neither flesh nor fleshless." It's the point where it turns from flesh to fleshless as it were. The zero point. "Neither from nor towards." If it's neither from nor towards, it's again the turning between the movement from and the movement towards, and this again is still.

Neither arrest nor movement. Neither standstill nor movement. What is that, that is neither standstill nor movement? It's the point between. It's like what the Zen masters say when they teach you the *mudra*. You hold your hands like this: the two thumbs should neither touch nor be separated. And then you sit there, always making sure that they are neither touching nor separated! That can keep you occupied for a while! That's also the still point, exactly; that's why they do it — it fits right in there.

Does it make sense to you that the whole world literature of poetry should spend so much time and energy on this?

When you really experience — that is when you are not reflecting on it and writing about it...because when you start writing about it, you have lost the experience, and you can only remember — that's really the crux of poetry, and the crux of writing poetry, I suppose. And that is why it's such a rare thing to find really good poetry. How do poets help themselves out of this dilemma?

Usually when I look for poems, I look for very short poems, because the chance of finding a good poem that is short is ten times better than finding a long poem that is good. The shorter it is, the better the chance that you will really catch it ... especially in the nineteenth century, when certain expectations were set up, and a poem had to have so many stanzas and so forth. Sometimes you come across a poem that has a marvelous first line, but from then on it's all padding. ... Why didn't the poet leave it at that? It was fine!

Haiku Is Always about Silence

Haiku poetry makes the same point. Now haiku is not really our form here in the West; so what we write here in the West is not really haiku — even at its best it's not really haiku. But there is a great deal of so-called haiku being written now, and it makes very interesting reading. There is already a second edition of *The Haiku Anthology* — I think the first volume came out about a decade earlier. These are the only haiku that were directly written in English. Remember that haiku was originally a Japanese form and had a lot to do with Zen — both come out of the same spirit — exactly capturing the still point, which is what it's all about. The words are only a kind of scaffolding around that silence. The center of a haiku is always silence, every haiku is about silence. The key to a haiku is always silence.

The first haiku anthology consisted only of haiku that had been written originally in English. But most if not all of the haiku had seventeen syllables arranged in three lines, very much like the Japanese, and tried to be faithful to that model. But seventeen syllables in three lines — five-seven-five — is mostly just external structure. In a real Japanese haiku there are so many connections, allusions to other haiku, to famous poets and to all sorts of other things; for instance, a Japanese reading a haiku always knows what season it happened in because there is a *season* word in it. There *must* be a season word so that you know exactly whether it's spring, summer, autumn, or winter. These are just the most superficial details; there are *countless* little details that you could never imitate in English. It has to be about nature — that is the most basic thing in Japan.

In the *second* haiku edition, you'd have a hard time finding even *one* that has even three lines with seventeen syllables because the poets have now completely switched, saying, "In English, it's just very different." Many still arrange them in three lines, but others arrange them in five lines, or in one line, and there's one that is even just one word! I like it! I think it's very interesting, it captures that moment.

But people now write other poems. I think the principle is that a haiku simply uses as few words as necessary to convey the silence of the still point. That's the idea.

Living in the Now

Most of the time we are ahead of ourselves, and we are not really here. Or we are 51 percent ahead of ourselves and 49 percent behind, and one percent present where we are, so we are not really in the Now. We are already anticipating what's going to happen, or we are still hanging on to something that is no longer happening. And sometimes we are really present where we are. That is the Now. As I said yesterday, Now has no plural. You can say, "the now" and "I am in the now," but you cannot say, "We are in the nows" or "I have several nows" or anything similar, because Now is *always* now. Whenever you experience this, you are in that realm of Now, of presence. Therefore, every single moment has the potentiality of being this Now. The whole spiritual quest is to live in this Now, to be present in this Now. It is not waiting around until the next Now happens. Now is *Now*! Few people — maybe no one — can be so alert and so awake that they are always present to everything. We just go along, and don't push ourselves, and every so often something flashes up — the eye of the little puppet that's hanging out, or the toenails of the dog on the floor, or the wind in the sailor's face — whatever it is, all these things sort of flash out.

As you go around Esalen — this is one of the reasons I like to do poetry workshops here — you'll find that it's one of those places where it is made very easy for you... there's a whale coming out of the water! Well, if that doesn't wake you up! Or there's a seal barking — how often do you hear a seal barking? Or something like that. And then there are these wonderful flowers. Just allow something to wake you up. Then try to live from that point. And the next moment when you're responding to someone, try to respond from that moment. We'll come back to that again and again and again.

Wherever you have good poetry, it's always about that still point. We will read other poems, and it will be a challenge to see how a poem that's a page long can still really be about that still point. I call it both "the still point" and "the turning point." This morning something occurred to me that I had never connected it with before.

Whenever you look at a simple chair that a Shaker made — or a table, a vessel, a broom, and so forth — it wakes you up. Because the Shakers were so fully awake. There is a Shaker song, probably the most famous of their melodies, that Copland used in *Appalachian Spring:*

To turn, to turn shall be our delight
So that by turning and turning we come 'round right.

Obviously, that's why they could do the things they did and
live the life they lived, because they were continuously concerned with this turning. That would be one way to understand
the turning point. When we speak of "the still point" — another
image is the swing. At the highest point — that's the point where
the going up and the coming down are in perfect balance — it
stands still for a moment. Remember when as kids you were in
a swing and you reached this point, where did you feel it? Here
in your *hara*, what the Japanese call your *hara*. That is your
turning point. That is your still point. That's the point when
we live moment by moment in the Now. We live then in this
hara, because all this is integrated with the body. That still point
is not something in your *head*; it's in your body. Dancers for
example, good dancers, will move from this still point. We tend
to move from our feet or from our shoulders. A dancer moves
from the *hara*, and everything else just revolves around that.

Hara is a Japanese term, and it means a place that's about
two inches — depending on your size — below your navel. It's
the center of your body, the center of your body *energy*. The
Japanese martial arts are all concerned with the *hara*. Not just
moving from the *hara*, but *perceiving* with the *hara*. When you
perceive not with your eyes or with your brain, but with your
hara, you can look around corners, and you know who is coming from behind. If somebody lifts up a weapon behind you,
you are aware that somebody is there. Why would that be? Just
as Now is always Now, and there is only one Now, there is
only one *hara*, and if you are there, you know exactly what
everybody else is doing. Does that make sense?

If you write a poem from your *hara* instead of from your head, it will touch everybody, because it will touch everybody else's *hara*. You make music from your *hara*, not from your fingers. You dance from your *hara* and you paint from your *hara*, and so on....

Now that we have an idea of what the still point is, the question is how do we cultivate it, and how can poetry help us cultivate it? I can only talk about this, of course, from my own experience. One could tackle this in millions of ways. I'm just telling you about my own way, how I do it, and how I practice it.

Blessing

Over the course of this workshop, Brother David discusses various aspects of the practice fostered by the contemplation of poetry. These are "Blessing, Response, and Aliveness," which he illustrates through poems by a range of poets, including W. H. Auden, Yeats, David Ignatow, Kathleen Norris, and Marge Piercy. What follows is his discussion of a poem by one of his favorite poets, the nineteenth-century English Jesuit Gerard Manley Hopkins.

Here is an important poem by Gerard Manley Hopkins. He was a nineteenth-century poet, a wonderful poet, whose poems are usually quite explicitly religious. Even people who share none of his religious convictions just lap them up and lick their lips because they are so good as poems. For thirty years after his death, his poems were not published, and not known — no one knew anything about them. They were published at the beginning of the twentieth century and became enormously influential. Practically our whole poetic tradition is influenced by Hopkins, in one way or another. Technically he's very, very important.

This is one of his sonnets. As it doesn't have a title, it is usually listed under the first words of the first line.

As Kingfishers Catch Fire
by G. Manley Hopkins

As kingfishers catch fire, dragonflies draw flame;
As tumbled over rim in roundy wells
Stones ring; like each tucked string tells, each hung bell's
Bow swung finds tongue to fling out broad its name;
Each mortal thing does one thing and the same:
Deals out that being indoors each one dwells;
Selves — goes itself; *myself* it speaks and spells,
Crying *What I do is me: for that I came.*

In the first part of this poem he mentions different things or animals — and always says what they do. Kingfishers are a kind of bird with very bright feathers. They often live in swamps, and at sunset when it begins to get dark, they have a habit of flying up and suddenly catching fire when they come into that region above the trees where there is still sunlight. We observe that. For Hopkins, as for each one of us, other words stand out in our memory. For him this is one of those particular words, this kingfisher, this bird. Kingfishers catch fire — that's what it does for him. That's its essence.

Dragonflies draw flame;

On a summer day when these dragonflies zip by, it looks almost as if they had a jet stream of flame behind them. That's the word of the dragonfly, that's what the dragonfly says. Without words it draws flame. That's what it does or says. And then comes this long sentence, so typically Hopkins:

> As tumbled over rim in roundy wells
> Stones ring;

As children we always wanted to throw stones into wells, those roundy wells with those rims; we always threw stones in, because we wanted to listen to what they *do* when they go down there. Little stones go *plip* and big ones go *plop* and there are all kinds of variations in between. We wanted to *hear* this. That's probably why he brings this in, because each stone has its own little word to say when it's thrown into the well. That's another element. So he is lifting words: kingfisher, dragonfly, stones in the well. And another one:

> . . . like each tucked string tells,

Every string on the harp, on the piano, on the lute, has its own word to say.

> . . . each hung bell's
> Bow swung finds tongue to fling out broad its name;

What a beautiful sentence. "Each hung bell's bow swung finds tongue to fling out broad its name." You can almost hear those bells ringing. Each bell has a different name and says that as it is being rung. And then, after he has made this whole list, he draws the conclusion, very elaborately, very explicitly, over and over again:

> Each mortal thing does one thing and the same:

That's the message. What is it that each mortal thing does, that one thing and the same that each mortal thing does?

Deals out that being which indoors each one dwells.

That's what each mortal thing does, it deals out that being which indoors each one dwells.

The poet Wallace Stevens has this marvelous prose line, *"There is always a poem at the heart of things."* That still point at the heart of everything that is, is a poem. There's *always* a poem at the heart of things. So that word is the poem that each thing deals out, that being which indoors each one dwells. And the poet is the one that has ears. The poet in us is the one who has ears to hear that word. Hopkins says it once more:

Each mortal thing does one thing and the same:
Deals out that being which indoors each one dwells;

Now he says it with one word: Selves. He had to coin this word for what each thing does: Each thing *selves*. Now he has to explain what he means by "selves." He does that:

Goes itself.

He says it once more:

Myself! It speaks and spells,
Crying, "What I do is me! For that I came!"

This is very complex language, but it's perfectly clear once you read it. It couldn't be said with fewer words. It couldn't really be said differently to get the same thing across. The second stanza, much shorter, but very important, begins with

I say more: the just man justices;

Keeps grace: that keeps all his goings graces;
Acts in God's eye what in God's eye he is —
Christ — for Christ plays in ten thousand places,
Lovely in limbs, and lovely in eyes not his
To the Father through the features of men's faces.

Each thing selves. For this I came. This is me. For this I came.

I say more:

Now that may mean "Wait a moment. I have more to say. This is not all." Or it may mean, "I as a human say *more* than all those things that simply selve." And this is what he says:

I say more: The just [one] justices.

Another coinage for him, you see.

The just [one] justices.

There's where your work comes in, where another standard comes in. Because "to justice" means that you take your stand, your ideals, your values, from something higher than yourself. You don't just say, "There I am. For this I came. This is me." No! I came to justice, I came to rise up to standards that I can perceive and the cat cannot, and to which I have to rise. I have to rise up to who I am. I cannot just blindly "be myself" and that's it.

Now "to justice" sounds a little moralistic and a little dry and so forth. Immediately, he feels that and he turns it into a completely different image: now it's dancing.

The just one justices;
Keeps grace:

Remember all the things that we said about grace? The just one keeps grace. Keeps grace. Keeps pace. Dances gracefully. That is all in this one thing.

> the just man justices;
> Keeps grace: that keeps all his goings graces;

You see? That we justice, that we listen to that music, that we keep pace with the rhythm in the dance. That keeps all our goings graces, and graceful. Not that we simply *are*. We justice, we listen, we keep grace: that keeps all our goings graces. And then he says the same thing once more:

> Acts in God's eye what in God's eye he is —
> Christ —

That is obviously not simply Jesus. Christ here stands for that divine reality, for that human divine reality, for that inner-most divine core of each one of us. The "Christ Reality" as we say nowadays, which might very well be based on Hopkins. He coined many of those expressions. For instance, everybody knows the phrase "Ground of Being" — if you want to be very polite in multireligious company you don't refer to God, you refer to the "Ground of Being" — and most people give the credit for having invented the phrase to Paul Tillich. But it goes straight back to Hopkins. He was the first one to use "Ground of Being." "Granite Shore" he calls it also. Ground of being, granite shore. And so:

> I say more: the just man justices;
> Keeps grace: that keeps all his goings graces;
> Acts in God's eye what in God's eye he is —
> Christ —

Now he has said everything he has to say, so he just winds it up and brings it all back to where we started out:

... for Christ plays in ten thousand places,
Lovely in limbs, and lovely in eyes not his

Not his!

To the Father ...

This is a sudden twist. He plays — but he plays to the Father. Like a musician. ... Up to that point we might think he was just playing. But he plays to the Father, so he's now playing the harp or some instrument.

plays in ten thousand places,
Lovely in limbs, and lovely in eyes not his
To the Father through the features of men's faces.

Each human face is another variation on this Christ Reality that he's speaking about. That still point. Always now, it's always the one still point, the Christ Reality. That is simply the term he uses. But each face is a different variation, it's not a sort of uniform cosmic jelly. ... Each one is *most unique,* and the *more* we become that, the more unique each one of us becomes: unmistakably unique.

There is a parallel then to that wonderful saying of Wallace Stevens: "There is always a poem at the heart of things." A great Lutheran theologian of our century, Oscar Cullmann, says there is "faithfulness at the heart of all things," which is almost exactly parallel.

Faithfulness. It's a poem, it is faithfulness, it's that still point. It is at that heart that we need the faithfulness of the source, the never-drying-out source of that fountain where we meet that faithfulness. Our faith, our trust in life, and our courage to go on — that is what faith is; it is not *believing* something; faith is *trust in life,* courageous trust in life — that faith is simply the response to the faithfulness which is at the heart of all things. That is spirituality, that's coming alive. That's all the things that we are about here.   — "Enjoying Poetry'

O GAIA:
NATURE AND POETIC INTUITION

Few people know that Benedictine monks do not make vows of poverty, celibacy, and obedience. They do vow obedience. That is correct. But their other two vows are *conversatio morum* and *stabilitas loci.* The first of these obliges the monk to an ever continued conversion, an ever repeated renewal of his life, an unceasing yielding to the formative power of monastic living. Thus, poverty and celibacy are here implied. *Stabilitas loci* (literally: "stability of place" or "local stability") is a vow which offers a timely starting point for tackling our topic and the question it poses. Our answer will have bite if we avoid generalities. This will be easiest if we start from a clearcut point of view. You will allow me, as a Benedictine monk, to make this uniquely Benedictine vow my starting point, even though my friends tease me about having stretched Local Stability, in my travels, to distant parts of the earth. Well, looking at things from a distance sometimes makes us see the essential features more clearly.

What, then, is the meaning of Local Stability? Its central concern is with being truly present where we are. This concern is common to monastic traditions throughout the world.

Most of us tend to be present with only a small portion of ourselves. A larger portion may still be clinging to the past and with another part we may be ahead of ourselves, impatiently reaching out for the future. But, since the only moment for action is now, spiritual training implies an effort to be present here now. Surprisingly, this goal can be achieved by methods that seem to contradict each other. Their extreme forms would be always traveling. Historical forms reach from extreme to extreme. Christian tradition knows St. Brendan the Seafarer and other Irish monks who were vowed to continuous travels, abandoning themselves in small boats to the currents of the sea. And over against them stands St. Simeon the Stylite, who spent thirty years atop a pillar. Between these two extremes are many different degrees of cutting loose and of taking roots, all of them aiming at the same result: to make the monk fully present wherever he is.

In St. Benedict's sixth-century Italy, the wandering monks had become a bit decadent. St. Benedict speaks of their restless round of monasteries. They stayed three or four days in each, and in his wording there is just the slightest hint to suggest that the length of their stay depended on how well they liked the food. (For our own monastery-hoppers today, the travel section of the *New York Times* offered, not long ago, helpful hints complete with clues to the menu.) By introducing Local Stability, St. Benedict went far beyond correcting monastic abuses. This new vow had unforseeable consequences. It turned out to be literally epoch-making. It turned Benedictine monasteries into stabilizing centers in Western society, and the epoch in which this took place is sometimes called the Benedictine centuries (eighth–twelfth).

When one becomes a Benedictine monk, one joins a particular monastery and belongs to it, normally, for the rest of one's life. In contrast to other orders in the Church, the Order of St. Benedict is simply a confederation of autonomous monasteries. In some monasteries the vow of Local Stability is interpreted in a strictly residential sense. In others it is seen to allow for travels, under obedience. Always, however, this vow roots the monk for life in one specific place, in one particular community. And that local community extends to the angels (or nature spirits), the neighbors, the animals, and plants of that area. This is where the relevance of Benedictine stability for our environmental concerns comes into view.

The Dark Ages of Europe were a time of utter uprootedness. In this they resembled our own times more than any other period in history. When we read an account like Christopher Dawson's *The Making of Europe,* this resemblance may come as a shock. At a closer look, however, we discern also a force of renewal during that period, which could renew our own culture: Local Stability. Its opposite is not mobility, as we might think, but uprootedness. This distinction between mobility and uprootedness is of importance. Mobility is not an evil, but a high achievement. To be able to travel easily, quickly, and safely is a great benefit. We can cultivate this good without being swept away by it. What threatens our times is not mobility, but uprootedness.

The roots that kept the Dark Ages from being swept away in a tide of violence were the roots of monastic stability. Monasteries, too, were vandalized and burnt to the ground again and again. But again and again they would be rebuilt in the same spirit and — a most important fact — in the same place. The monks replanted their orchards, restored their mills, and remembered local lore. That was decisive. It gave cult, culture, and agriculture the necessary anchorage. There is no reason why monasteries cannot play a similar role today. Some do. Families that were attached to our monastery, but had to move, will sometimes come back year after year, even clear across the continent. Their only real home is with us. Monks must rise to that responsibility. But that won't be enough. Millions will have to rise to their responsibility, commit themselves, and take roots again locally. What agonies of decision this can cause for parents who have to choose between economic advancement linked to a transfer and their children's needs for Local Stability.

Children do have that need. Some qualities of the human psyche will simply never develop unless one grows up in a stable family — one that is stable also in a local sense. We speak of growing up. Why do we never speak of "growing down"? Because roots don't matter to us. They are just that dirty mess that is inevitably attached down below to what we really admire. But when we put an avocado pit in water to let it sprout, we notice that it grows down before it grows up. And for a long time so. Not until the roots are well developed do the first leaves appear. This is nature's way. It is ingrained in us humans, too. But children are incredibly adaptable. If they have to change schools every other year, they will adjust. They will get used somehow to making new friends, again and again, if they must. It will leave scars. But they will compensate for the loss. Children of army personnel and of parents in the diplomatic service are sometimes good examples for this. We humans can weather many abuses. Our natural environment, however, must pay the price.

A friend of mine went back to visit his grandmother's farm, where he had grown up as a child. His family had lived in that place since colonial times, but they had all moved away, and the grandmother had long since died. Where was the farm? Where was the old swimming hole at the rock spring? "It is probably a wet spot in someone's basement now," my friend said with a bitter smile. "They cut down the pine forest to the last trees and bulldozed right over the spring. But why?" He answered his own question: "There was no one left to tell them where to stop." Newcomers don't. Every place on earth has its ecological problems today. If we are merely transients, we won't even be aware of these problems. We will have no eyes for the grassroots solutions. Nor will we have the drive and stamina to labor for those solutions, unless we make the personal investment of committing ourselves to a given place. Staying-power is what counts.

But there is more to it. Having roots in a place helps taking root in one's own depth. For the span of a lifetime now, my friends Art and Nan Kellam have been living alone on an outer island in Maine. When a visitor asked if they ever got struck by wanderlust, Art simply said, "When you can't go far, you go deep." That is the direction to which Benedictine monks commit themselves by their vow of Local Stability. It should make them sink their roots into that inner depth where the great images of myth and poetry come alive.

Since poetry has so small an audience, the notion has begun to grow up that it is a kind of survival from more primitive times, a form of communication no longer needed by modern people. The fact is rather that modern people are something like a survival of poetry, which once shaped and interpreted our world through language and the creative imagination. When poetry withers in us,

> the greater part of experience and reality wither too; and when this happens, we live in a desolate world of facts, not of truth — a world scarcely worth the trouble of living in.

This perceptive passage by the Australian poet Judith Wright gives us a key to our problem. Poetry has withered in us. The environmental abuses we perpetuate all over the world are largely the results of poetry starvation. It is not only that "poetry takes the violence out of reason," as J. F. Kennedy put it. Poetry gives us access to those reasons of the heart which reason cannot fathom. Only the poet within each of us has eyes for the inherent sacredness of nature.

John Henry Newman characterized the Benedictine tradition as the poetic thread woven into the history of the great orders in the Church. Seen through the eyes of this tradition, the problem stated in our topic calls for an educational rather than a legislative solution. The answer to our question will have to be evocative rather than provocative. *How can we make the intuitive knowledge of the sacredness of nature an effective force in the world?* By exposing ourselves to the *sacredness of nature* through a stable commitment to the place where we live, and by rooting ourselves in the realm of *intuitive knowledge* through poetry. The educational implications could be revolutionary. The effective force released could be momentous.

When education is at its best, it frees within us our own effective force to become who we truly are. The biblical prototype for who we humans are is Adam — Adam, formed out of the very soil of the garden in which he lives, and where he gives names to all creatures. Adam, the Earthling, the Human, is both gardener and poet. In the history of Benedictine education the image of Adam plays a central role. I remember entering the great lecture hall at the University of Salzburg, in the shadows of an ancient Benedictine abbey, and there, on a wall-hanging above the rostrum, was the image that gathered up the significance of the whole institution: Adam in the garden, naming the animals.

Adam in the Garden of Eden bears the likeness of God, whose image he is. But the Old Adam becomes a warped mirror, as it were. The New Adam, Jesus Christ, restores in himself the image to its original likeness. In the Garden of Olives the bloody sweat of Jesus irrigates the earth. And on Easter morning the risen Christ is at first mistaken for a gardener. We never cease to be an image of God, disfigured though this image may have become. By the labor of obedience we can return to the one from whom we strayed in lazy disobedience, and the image will regain the splendor of its likeness. Adam means "human." And so, each one of us is meant to be poet and gardener. The more human we become, the more fully we become image and likeness of God. But God is both Poet and Gardener.

To speak of God in these terms may strike us as fanciful. In fact, the way some people talk could make one think of God as accountant or policeman rather than as poet or gardener. Could this be the result of the warped mirror within ourselves? All around us, nature bears abundant proof that God's creation springs from the playful work of a gardener. God does not labor like a farmer. God plays. And all of history proves that God likes to spin a good yarn, poetically. What should give us a clue is the uselessness of it all. Why do we tend to overlook how useless God's creation is to God? Poorly remembered, the story in the Book of Genesis makes us think that God worked hard to achieve a purpose. But what could that purpose have been?

Was God in need of anything? The pattern on a goldfinch's wing should be enough to convince anyone that it was all play. And the story of creation is told in such a way as to leave no doubt: it was all as effortless for God and as joyful as the whistling of a shepherd boy stretched out on the hillside and looking into the summer sky.

God plays. Work always has a purpose. But there is no purpose to nature and history. And yet, it all is filled with deep meaning. Thank God, there is no purpose to the world! That is why it is truly a world without end. Work comes to an end when its purpose is accomplished. Who would go on drawing water, once all the vessels are filled to the brim? But to play now that this water is wine: that is divine make-believe. Or to play that whosoever drinks from it will never thirst again; that, sprinkled on you, it can make you whiter than snow; that you can go down into it, die, and come up more alive than before — those are games you can go on playing, world-without-end. Play has no purpose, only meaning. And there is no end to meaning. Once we open our eyes to this, we won't be concerned with "discovering the *purpose* of human life." Rather, we will celebrate its meaning. That will give us joy and strength enough to take care of all those purposes for which we are responsible on the level of work as if they were play. And this will lead to results that last.

Did I hear a voice there in the corner, meekly asking, "But how?" Well, let us formulate a check list of questions to help us translate these reflections into action. (Please note that these questions apply regardless of where you live, even in the city. Answering them should not be work, but play, and you can turn it into a game, if you and a friend do it together.)

- *What place can you call home in the full sense of the word?*

- *How much time do you spend there? How much of it outdoors?*

- *How many flowers, grasses, trees that grow there do you know by name?*

- *What do you know about the mammals, birds, fish, reptiles, insects of your neighborhood? Their names? Their living habits?*

- *How many of your neighbors do you know by name? First name? Last name? The names of their children? Of their pets?*

- *How would you rate your relationship to your neighbors? Distant? Cordial? Cooperative?*

- *Do you ever discuss with your neighbors questions concerning the environment you share and its protection?*

- *When did you last sit or walk outdoors without a specific purpose, just looking, listening, doing nothing?*

- *Do you grow anything? In a garden? In flower pots or planters?*

- *Name the three most pressing environmental problems of your neighborhood, your country, your state or region.*

- *Who are your political representatives: What are their positions on environmental issues?*

- *What is your opinion of the significance of poetry in human life? In education?*

- *What place does poetry occupy in your own life?*

- *Name two books of the Bible whose literary form is poetry. Do you think one can get the gist of the teachings of Jesus (especially the parables in the gospels) without a sense for poetry?*

- *Name three poets whose work you personally enjoy (not just think you ought to enjoy).*

- *Name one poet whose work you enjoy less, or not at all. Give reason why.*

- *Who is your favorite poet?*

- *Do you know who your closest friend's favorite poet is?*

- *Do you ever read poems with your friends? Your children?*

- *Which poet or poem had a significant influence on your inner development?*

- *When did you last sit down to read a poem for enjoyment?*

- *Roughly, how many poems do you know by heart? Recite one.*

—Reprinted from *Epiphany*, Spring 1983

6

Love — A "Yes" to Belonging

The quest of the human heart for meaning is the heartbeat
of every religion.   — *GHP, 35*

*In the following excerpts we glean fascinating glimpses of what
shamans mean when they teach that "we are all one." We
belong together. We breathe — oxygen in, carbon dioxide out.
A tree breathes in carbon dioxide and breathes out the oxygen
that keeps all animals alive, including us. As has been frequently
stressed in recent months, what we do to our environment, we
do to ourselves. Brother David has much to say about the great
"Yes" to belonging, as an expression of love; both in mystical
traditions across the religious spectrum and in belonging to the
universe. Are they the same thing?*

THE CHRISTIAN MYSTICAL TRADITION
AND THE EARTH HOUSEHOLD

That we belong is a given fact. This means that it is both fact
and gift. Belonging is *the* basic fact. All other facts rest on
belonging. And it is *the* basic gift. Every other gift celebrates, in

its own way, belonging. Belonging is mutual and all-inclusive. Whatever there is belongs to whatever else there is. Every longing somehow longs to realize belonging more fully and thus more fully to be. Because belonging is a fact, we are at home in the world, wherever we may find ourselves. And because belonging is a gift, gratefulness is the right response to life, whatever happens.   — *GHP*, 193

When we lift our hearts to God, whom we call "Our Father in heaven," we see that we belong to a household that embraces all creatures, the Earth Household in Gary Snyder's powerful poetic term. And if we put our hands to work in service of that Earth Household, this contemplative matching of vision by action will spread God's peace "on earth as it is in heaven." The crucial question is: How big is our family? How wide is the reach of our belonging? Can we stretch it to the furthest reaches of God's household? Will our care and concern stretch to embrace all members of this Earth Household — humans, animals, plants, whom we now still consider strange? The survival of all of us may well depend on our answer.
                    — *GHP*, 184

It is the concept of self that expands when we come to understand what love really means. The current idea of love identifies our self with our little individualistic ego. This little ego translates "Love thy neighbor as thyself" into a series of incredible mental acrobatics. Step one: imagine you are someone else. Step two: try to whip up a passionate attraction for that imaginary other. Step three: Try to feel for someone who is really someone else the same passionate attraction you felt for yourself (if you did) when you were imagining that you were someone else.

That's asking a little much, isn't it? And yet the command is so simple: "Love your neighbor as (being) yourself." That means: realize that your self is not limited to your little ego. Your true self includes your neighbor. You belong together — radically so. If you know what self means, you know what belonging means. It costs you no effort to belong to yourself. Spontaneously, you say "yes" to yourself in your heart. But at heart you are one with all others. Your heart knows that your true self includes our neighbor. Love means that you say "yes" from your heart to that true self — and act accordingly.   — *GHP*, 168–69

Growing in love means drawing out the implications of that "yes" which our heart sings out spontaneously when we are at our best. But drawing out these implications is not an easy task. Falling in love happens by itself; rising to the heights of love costs an effort.... It demands determination to rebuff the big wind, to bridle up when indifference threatens to overpower us. Falling in love is barely the beginning of a great love. The glimpses we catch of our great, blissful belonging are merely a challenge to growth in relationships, a challenge to grow to our full human nature. Only on the wings of love will we rise to that challenge.   — *GHP*, 173–74

We grow in love when we grow in gratefulness. And we grow in gratefulness when we grow in love....

We know that our deepest joy springs from living in love. The key to that joy is the "yes" which love and gratefulness have in common. Thanksgiving is the setting in which that "yes" is most naturally practiced. This makes gratefulness a school in which one learns love. The only degrees one receives in that school are degrees of aliveness. With every "yes" one relationship or another grows deeper and broader. And aliveness can only be measured by the intensity, depth, and variety of our relationships. If the fullness of gratitude which the word "gratefulness" implies can ever be reached, it must be fullness of love and fullness of life.   — *GHP*, 176–77

RELATIONALITY

It is fitting that Brother David received the 1975 Martin Buber award for his achievements in building bridges between religious traditions. Martin Buber, the famous author of I and Thou, *wrote that human beings are ultimately constituted as subjects by the quality of their relationship to others — whether nature, other people, or the Eternal Thou. After intense study of the Hasidim, Buber concluded that they represented a "worldly holiness," an attention to those sparks of the divine that lie hidden within the challenges and responsibilities of the present moment. How fitting that a book about Martin Buber was called* The Way of Response, *ed. Nahum N. Glatzer (New York: Schocken, 1966) as that is an extraordinarily apt description of Brother David's journey as well. Relationality and response are recurring themes in his exploration of the heart of the Christian message.*

In an interview with Kate Olson of the Fetzer Institute, in which they talk about the way of love in the Christian tradition, Brother David expounds further on relationality:

The term "relationality" came up in a conversation with Raimundo Panikkar in terms of emergence. Relationality is dynamic. This dynamism is absolutely essential. The celebration of that relationship which is love, this is what Christians now call the

Holy Spirit. There the relationship between the gift and the giver is thanksgiving. Thanksgiving and love in this respect are one and the same. Loving is a form of thanksgiving. Living is a form of thanksgiving. Knowing is a form of thanksgiving. Searching, exploring, in this context of knowing, is a form of thanksgiving. Our devotion is thanksgiving. All this and this spirit of thanksgiving is itself divine.

All of this takes us back to the Christian tradition, which is capable of embracing this wider God image if it wakes up to it. If nowhere else, it's beginning to wake up in me.

Now our understanding of the Trinity is no longer as it still is in the Christian catechism, somewhere whirling around up there, separated from us.... Now we have a completely different God image — not the God separated from us, but the panentheistic God, in whom we are totally immersed and who is totally in us, and in whom we "live and move and have our being," as St. Paul said long ago. He did not say this to the Christians, to whom he expressed himself in different terms, but to the pagans. "We live and move and have our being" is a quote from Paul speaking in Athens.... It's quite interesting. Not that he would have withheld it from the Christians, but he recognized that that was a different context....

When we find our true self, we can say with e.e. cummings, "I am through you so I." This is an extremely important sentence. "I am through you so I." That the "I" which we discovered, this true self that can say "I" in a full and deep sense, is not its own source, but a gift. We are gift. We are receiving ourselves from a mystery that goes beyond all that we can conceive. So we receive ourselves.

— Originally posted at *www.fetzer.org*
under Publications and Resources

JESUS AND SALVATION

Jesus didn't go around saying, "Here is my message that I bring to you from God." He didn't speak like the prophets, who said, "Thus speaks the Lord." Instead, he taught with parables, asking "Who of you does not know this?" In other words, he placed the authority for his teaching in the hearts of his hearers. He rested his teaching on the divine authority, the ultimate authority, that spoke in the hearts of his hearers and that speaks in our own heart of hearts. "You know it already, don't you? Now act accordingly" — and that's basically what the parable says to us. It catches us sort of admitting we know the truth already. Jesus' messages and his teaching method were completely integrated." — *GWS*, 41

The profoundly Christian teaching that one should question authority has largely been lost. This is really one of the most basic teachings of Jesus. — *GWS*, 193

On Salvation

It all hinges, of course, on the question of what saving means. Long ago, when I was first studying with Eido Roshi, he made a distinction between two ways in which we use the word "saving." On the one hand, we speak about saving somebody who is drowning, pulling him out, saving his life. That's the kind of saving that most people have in mind when they speak about Jesus Christ as a savior. On the other hand, we commonly use the word in a different sense in phrases like saving water or saving energy and so forth. This means not wasting anything, or in positive terms, it means being keenly aware of the value of every drop of water, every bit of energy — affirming the value of these things. In both senses, it seems to me, both the Buddha and Jesus are saviors. As enlighteners, teachers, they save us from error in the first sense: they pull us out of the illusions and misconceptions in which we're lost. In the case of Jesus, it's clear, if you look at the gospels — not at what we teach about Jesus but at his teaching — that he's also a savior in the second sense. The essential point in his life, long before he dies on the cross, is that he affirms the value of every human being as a human being, very much to the distress of the authorities, who want to put those sinners and harlots and tax collectors down. He affirms the value of every human being as a human being and in that way saves them, by saving their self-respect, by making them stand on their own two feet and pulling them out of that consensus reality that their society had formed and that, sadly, hasn't changed very much in our society.

— *GWS*, 42–43

To spell out more fully what salvation means in a Christian context, we'd have to start where I started just a moment ago — by saying that Jesus saved people long before the cross was in view. He saved people by making them stand on their own two feet. That's how he was understood as a savior by his own contemporaries. He gave them back their self-respect and gave them back their deepest relationship — to God, to the Ultimate — by reminding them that it was never lost. With Jesus, it wasn't, "Here, I give it to you." He never said, "I forgive your sins." Jesus says, "Your sins are forgiven," with the implied "Don't you know that?" It's his adversaries who said, "Who's that guy to forgive people's sins? Only God can forgive sins."

Of course, the authorities of his time — the political authorities, together with authoritarian religious authorities — didn't
look kindly on his saving people this way, just as their equals in
Central America today don't look kindly on anyone who helps
people stand on their own two feet. It's pretty obvious from
the gospels, although one has to read them as late accounts of
something that happened much earlier, that his saving activity
was leading toward the cross and that Jesus willingly took this
upon himself as a free, willing sacrifice for his cause, for what
he stood for, and as a gesture of trusting God.

— *GWS*, 44–45

On Resurrection

After [Jesus] was put away by the establishment, his followers,
although at first shattered and scattered, recognized that this
kind of life can't be extinguished.... That's what we call resurrection. It's presented to us in mythical imagery, and we can't
unravel events to determine what happened historically.... It
is something that happens today in countless lives and can be
experienced: he freed us. Christ lives in those who follow his
path, and they live in him; that's the ultimate kind of salvation. They are alive with his life and, in turn, become saviors
for others.   — *GWS*, 45

The life of Jesus is so important. In the way Jesus lives he takes
an anti-authoritarian stance in the world, and that stance grows
out of his mystic intimacy with God. Looking at Jesus, we see
how one lives when one has this mystic intimacy with God,
when one says yes to limitless belonging. That's what he lives.
If one lives this way in the kind of world we have created, one

will be squelched or in one way or the other crucified. Now the question arises, Is that the end? The teaching of the resurrection is the affirmation that it's not the end. This kind of aliveness cannot be extinguished. He died, he really died, and behold, he lives!

Where does he live? Let's not make the mistake of saying he is here or there. No. A rarely cited early Christian answer is this: "His life hidden in God." Paul doesn't say it in these words; he says, "*Our* life is hidden *with Christ* in God." But that implies that Christ's life is hidden in God. God's presence in this world is hidden, and yet it is the most tangible thing for anybody who lives with full awareness. God's presence is everywhere; still, it is a hidden presence. Jesus died, and yet he is alive, and his life is hidden in God. He is also alive in us. There is no way of pointing a finger and saying, "Look!" or "Zap! He came out from the tomb." Resurrection is not revivification; it is not survival; it is not a matter of saying, "There he is!" It's a hidden reality, but it is a reality, and we can live in the strength of its power. And that's all we need to know about the resurrection.

—*BTU*, 65

The creed expresses basic human faith in Christian terms, just as Buddhists' beliefs are an expression of that same basic human faith common to all. Faith — courageous trust in the mystery of Life — makes us human, and each culture, each period of history, gives this faith new expressions in beliefs that are determined by historic and cultural circumstances. Beliefs divide, but the faith from which they spring is one and unites. The task of interreligious dialogue is to make our divergent beliefs transparent to the one Faith we share.   —*DTW*, 14

COURAGE

Let's think positively ... about our fears. We know that courage presupposes fear. This is true even with the courage of faith. ... There is a play, *The Song on the Scaffold,* based on a novel by Gertrud von LeFort, that tells of a community of Carmelite nuns during the French Revolution. Disobeying orders to abandon their religious life, the nuns are imprisoned and led to their execution. So great is their faith and courage that they go up to the scaffold singing. Their song gets softer and softer as one by one the women are beheaded. Only with the last one the song ends. But this is where the core of the story begins. For, as it turns out, the last one to die with her companions was not really the last.

One of the nuns had not had the courage to face death. She had gone into hiding. And now she must struggle all alone through agony after agony until she, too, gives herself up to be executed. To the last moment she is full of fear. But in the end it clearly emerges that her courage was greater than that of those who died triumphantly. Because the fear she had to overcome was so much greater, the courage that overcame her fear was greater too.

We might think of fear as the headwind of faith. The faster we go, say, on a bicycle, the stronger is the headwind we feel. It is our speed that creates that courage. As long as our faith remains a nose's length ahead of our fear, fine. Let's measure our courage by the fears we manage to master and pat ourselves on the back. We need not fear fear.

The struggle between fear and faith crystallizes into the image of Jesus in His agony. In the Garden of Olives, He becomes "the pioneer of our faith." But this trail-blazing costs

Him bloody sweat. In the end He accepts the cup just as He had accepted the stones in place of bread. Are we not invited to see a connection between this bread and cup and the bread and cup of the Lord's Supper? Whenever Christians celebrate the Eucharist, breaking bread and sharing the cup, they celebrate fullness of life. Yes, but with reference to death, with reference to a bloody agony in which faith conquered fear. The Eucharist is a challenge to follow Christ from fear to faith.

The very symbols of the Eucharistic meal are ambiguous symbols. Bread is a symbol of life. The breaking of bread signifies sharing of life that grows in the sharing. And yet the breaking also signifies destruction; it is a reminder of the body broken in death. The cup of blood drained from the body signifies death. But it is also the cup passed around in a festive gathering of friends, in an hour celebrating life. It takes courage to accept this double meaning. Only together can the two aspects stand for fullness.

The courage it takes to receive life even under the image of death — that is the courage of faith, the courage of gratefulness: trust in the Giver. When one approaches the altar to receive the Eucharistic bread and cup, this is an act of courage. It is a gesture by which one says, "I trust that I can live by *every* word that comes from the mouth of God, yes, even the word that spells death." All that remains is to translate that act of faith into daily living. And this is done through gratefulness. Eucharist, after all, means "thanksgiving." As we learn to give thanks for all of life and death, for all of this given world of ours, we find a deep joy. It is the joy of courageous trust, the joy of faith in the faithfulness at the heart of all things. It is the joy of gratefulness in touch with the fullness of life.

— *GHP,* 119–22

ASCETICISM

[We need to] correct a tendency to give first place to renunciation when we think of asceticism. No. Delight must come first.... Too often ascetic practice is presented not as learning wholehearted attention, but as fitting into some mold of abstinence; not as joyful attunement of all our senses, but as their rejection. Thus, asceticism becomes "mortification" — literally "killing" — instead of life-affirming listening with a grateful heart.

This can lead to dreadful distortions. No wonder we find a healthy hesitation even among spiritually serious people today when the topic of asceticism comes up. We have been misled too often. A sound intuition tells us: delight deserves first place and renunciation itself is merely a means for greater, more genuine delight. Bernard of Clairvaux, an ascetic if there ever was one, listed the benefits of fasting. On top of this list he put: "food tastes so much more delicious when you are hungry."

—LH, 52–53

THE EARTH HOUSEHOLD

Using the imagery of his Jewish tradition, Jesus calls his vision of a world in which harmony reigns "the kingdom of God."

In our age, kings belong to the realm of fairy tales. Obedience to a supreme ruler is no longer a value that inspires us. A pyramid of authority with king and god — or even God — on top is a defunct model; today's emerging model is closer to what Gary Snyder calls "Earth Household." Here, authority works from

within: the family spirit of Common Sense makes all work in
harmony with all.   — *WCS*, 42

The "kingdom" that Jesus envisages is a "God Household." He
sees God not so much as our king, but as our Father; and the
motherly Spirit (originally a feminine term) is an all-pervading
sense of family, our Common Sense. In the God Household,
the love of power yields to the power of love. "The smaller
the lizard, the greater its ambition to become a crocodile," they
say in Ethiopia. It's hard to assess if this is true among reptiles,
but it is certainly true among humans. The degree of power
one wields determines one's place in the authority pyramid of a
worldly kingdom. But the kingdom of heaven has the authority
structure of a household. Here, the mark of authority is service:
"Let the greatest among you become as the least, and the leader
as the one who serves" (Luke 22:26). In the God Household,
those in authority must use their power to empower all who are
under their authority.   — *WCS*, 42–43

*Belonging to the Universe, Explorations on the Frontiers of
Science and Spirituality* (1991) *traces new paradigm thinking
emerging in both science and theology. It consists of a dialogue
between the scientist Fritjof Capra and David Steindl-Rast, who
requested the help of Father Thomas Matus in drawing up a
parallel model for theology. Brother David must have really
relished these conversations, having always welcomed the intellectual sparks that can fly in dialogue with a small group of
people. Brother David writes in the Preface:*

The pages of this book bear the imprint of Big Sur with its
incomparable beauty. This ought to be an illustrated book. Yet

what illustrations could capture the changing light in the euca-
lyptus trees, the ever-changing coloration of sky and sea? What
could convey the fragrance of that garden perched on cliffs
above the sea, the sound of breakers thundering deep down
below? The warm, heavy smell of compost, the wind's sound
in the cypresses, the gurgling of the creek under the wooden
footbridge were so intimately interwoven with the mood of
our dialogues that readers might smell and feel and hear them
unawares. Wine tasters, after all, taste the soil in which the
grapes grew.

Although this setting in nature is not explicitly mentioned in
our text, it was an essential element of our conversations. The
sense of belonging, which lies at the heart of spiritual awareness, became the central theme of these intellectual encounters;
and having them in such a magnificent natural setting —
embedded in nature's cycles of light and darkness, of burning sun and soothing mist, of serene calmness and frightening
thunderstorms — made us experience that sense of belonging
more vividly than our most animated discussions. Our constant
shared experience of a dialogue not only among ourselves but
also with the Earth helped us again and again to reach intuitive
understandings and tacit agreements where words had to be left
behind.

We like to think that the Earth, our Great Mother, is present
on every page of this book.... Gaia, the living Earth, is the
silent source of everything we say in these conversations. She
gives us the context for the new thinking about God and
Nature.   — *BTU*, viii

As they begin the conversation, Fritjof Capra asks about the
relation of faith to theology:

Thomas:...Theology serves to make faith grow as a social reality, as a social experience.

Fritjof: But it also leads to a body of knowledge. That's what it has in common with science.

Brother David: This may be the point where we can start developing the parallel. I would start from the model making. I think it would be justified to say that theology is a human effort to make models that spring from our knowledge and exploration of the religious experience in the widest sense. Definitely, theological models, too, must be internally consistent. Sometimes they are not, and that calls for development and new models. Or we found them consistent in the past but no longer find them so. That leads to a paradigm shift, exactly as in science.

Then theological models, too, are only approximate. That is sometimes difficult for people to accept who invest so much effort in theology, and for church leaders who identify fidelity with adherence to particular models of faith. You know how difficult it is in science to remember that models are only approximate. When people are existentially as engaged as they are in theology, they tend to equate these insights with the whole truth.

Fritjof: I think it's very important to see that the notion of approximation is much more difficult in theology because of the existential engagement. The personal engagement of scientists can be pretty strong, too, but it's a different matter when you're existentially engaged, when your salvation depends on it.

Brother David: Salvation in the sense of realizing your connection to the whole, of real belonging; that is salvation. And salvation really means realizing your connection to the whole of the universe, your experience of being at home, feeling secure, truly belonging in some ultimate sense. Your finding your place in the cosmos depends on it, and so you tend to forget that it is only approximate.   — *BTU*, 26

Brother David: . . . We spoke about [the] sense of belonging. All the religions of the world would admit that this is our basic common ground. This is the experiential ground. So we have now established something that we could call God, if you want to use that term for the reference point of our ultimate belonging. God is the one to whom we ultimately belong.

Expressed in this way, this insight presupposes a long journey of exploration into God. It already presupposes the recognition that the reference point of our belonging must be personal. But of course God must not be restricted by any of the limitations we associate with being a person. One of those limitations is, for instance, that being me, I cannot at the same time be another. This does not apply to God. In other words, God must have all the perfection of being a person and none of the limitations.

Now, from there, it is again a long journey of exploration until we come to see that God freely allows us to belong, gives us this belonging. Up to this point, it was a sort of territory I was exploring, God-territory. But now all of a sudden I experience Yes! I am doing the exploring, but it isn't just my exploring, it is at the same time God's unveiling Godself. In the process of religious history, which stretches over millennia, this is a milestone. Yet every one of us can relive this experience. To explore into God is prayer, not in the conventional sense, but in the sense that theology is prayer. As we explore the God-territory prayerfully, we suddenly reach a point where we discover that it gives itself to us. God and the whole universe are giving themselves continuously to us.

Fritjof: So revelation, then, is really connected with the notion of the personal God?

Brother David: Yes, I do not think that the term "revelation" could make any sense except in that context.... It's a living process. We often use the term "God intervening" when we forget that it is a storytelling way of talking about revelation. God doesn't sit up there and then intervene occasionally. It's not so much an intervention on God's part as a discovery, a liberation, a new insight on our part.   —*BTU*, 27–28

Brother David: Since God is the self of ourselves, truth is always revealed by our deeper self. But I would be careful in using the term "revelation" too broadly. My emphasis when I speak of revelation falls on God's self-revealing. The correct image is not that of your pulling away a veil but of the bride unveiling herself for the bridegroom. That is the underlying image of revelation. Therefore it comes close to Heidegger's notion of truth, connected with the Greek word for truth.

Thomas: That word is *aletheia,* which means "unhiddenness": the truth deliberately "unhides" itself, lights itself up. This is something we all experience.... Revelation is the basis. Faith can be understood as *response* to revelation, a welcoming, an embracing.   —*BTU*, 29

Fritjof: And then theology is the intellectual exploration of that response. I think you could say that what we talked about earlier is the experience of belonging from *our* point of view. But if you belong to somebody, there is also the other point of view. And that would be revelation.

Brother David: That is the key word. There is a key word in the Psalms that seems to me to be one of those milestones of discovery: "O God, you are my God." O God, you are *my* God. You *belong* to me!

Fritjof: So the belonging is a two-way street.

Brother David: A two-way street! That is the tremendous discovery.

Fritjof: ... Now, when it filters down to the everyday life of the scientist, there is still a great difference between science and theology, because science is active exploring, not sitting there in prayer or meditation and allowing reality to reveal itself. Nevertheless, the whole attitude in science has been what Schumacher called a science of manipulation rather than a science of wisdom. What we want to recapture now is the science of wisdom, and maybe revelation will play a great role there.

Brother David: At least in Heidegger's sense that reality gives itself, unveils itself to us *deliberately.* And we are awestruck with this gift. It is available to everybody, to every human being. That is the main thing, the world gives itself to us. It gives itself freely to us, if we just allow it. It showers us with gifts.

— *BTU,* 29–30

Fritjof: Asceticism is part of the religious experience though.

Brother David: It doesn't bring about the religious experience, but it leaves you open for it. It prepares you for it. God's revelation, the breaking through of the divine reality into

our everyday reality, is something that is going on continuously. By making ourselves more perceptive to it, we receive
it. These various practices of making yourself perceptive are
asceticism.... Really what asceticism is all about (is): being in
the present moment mindfully and gratefully.   — *BTU*, 33

Regarding Ecology and Religion

Fritjof: ... Ecological awareness and ecological consciousness go
far beyond science, and at the deepest level they join with religious awareness and religious experience. Because at the deepest
level, ecological awareness is an awareness of the fundamental interdependence of all phenomena and of this embeddedness
in the cosmos. And, of course, the notions of being embedded
in the cosmos, and of belonging to the cosmos, are very similar. This is where ecology and religion meet. And this is also
why the new paradigm thinking in science has these surprising
parallels to thinking in spiritual traditions.... The worldview
now emerging from modern science is an ecological view, and
ecological awareness at its deepest level is spiritual or religious awareness. And this is why the new paradigm, within
science and even more outside it, is accompanied by a new
rise of spirituality, particularly a new kind of Earth-centered
spirituality.

Brother David: We see eye to eye on that one. I want to point
out another interesting parallel. Where you say, "ecological,"
we say "ecumenical." That is not only a play on words; it is
the deeper truth that in both cases we have the intuition of an
Earth Household, because the root of both terms is the Greek
word *oikos*, "house."

Fritjof: What are the implications?

Thomas: Well, *oikos* refers to the inhabited world, the house of humanity.

Brother David: To the "Earth Household" as Gary Snyder calls it.

Fritjof: Only to the human realm?

Brother David: No, no. We want to stress a wider belonging, not restricted to humans....

As often as possible, I try to use the term "Earth Household." It's such a good expression. Ecumenical and ecological are sort of abstract, sitting out there; but the moment you say Earth Household, there you have it.... The Pax Benedictina of the Middle Ages held the world together as an Earth Household, at least the way it was understood then. — *BTU*, 70–71

On the Individual vs. the Person

When Brother David is asked to say a little more about human freedom, he replies:

Brother David: In connection with our freedom, it helps to distinguish between the individual and the person. An *individual* is defined by what distinguishes it from other individuals: so many individual eggs in this crate; so many human individuals in this population.

A *person* is defined by the relationship to others, to other persons and to other beings in general. We are born as individuals, but our task is to become persons, by deeper and more intricate, more highly developed relationships. There is no limit to becoming more truly personal.

So the challenge to our freedom would be to personalize the universe. Before we arrive, the world is not yet personal. Adam encounters in the Garden an impersonal environment, but now he can make it personal. His giving names to the animals is one aspect of personalizing activity.

Fritjof: That is even stronger in the Native American traditions, where they not only give names but actual family relationships to all living things.

Brother David: Beautiful. And these myths are our common human heritage. They tell us what it means to be human.

—*BTU, 95*

TRANSFORMERS OF THE EARTH

As human beings we stand at the crossroads of body and mind, of senses and sense. To hold these opposite poles together in harmony is our existential task. Now and then, someone accomplishes this task and the result shines forth as uniquely human beauty: a body radiant with brightness from beyond the senses; intangible splendor yet fully embodied. The eyes of true lovers are lucid enough to see this beauty in each other; we catch glimpses of it in great masterpieces of the visual arts; a piece of music may express it, or a poem, or a dancer's grace. The Austrian poet Rainer Maria Rilke, who wrote his *Duino Elegies* and *Sonnets to Orpheus* in the same year (1922) in which T. S. Eliot wrote *The Wasteland,* made our standing at the crossroads a central theme of his poetic work. For Rilke, we humans stand at the crossroads between animals and angels. Angels are in Rilke's mythic worldview as completely at home in a realm beyond the senses, in "the invisible," as animals are in "the visible," the realm of the senses. Astride both domains stands Orpheus, representative of full human existence.

> Is he a local? No, from both
> Regions stems his vast nature.
> — *Sonnets to Orpheus,* 1:6

Being at home on both sides of the border, we humans are destined to be translators. We can teach angels who are eager to learn what only our animal senses can perceive. We humans alone can transform "the visible" into "the invisible." "We are transformers of the Earth," Rilke writes, "our whole existence... fits us for this task (a task to which no other stands comparison)."   — *LH,* 21–22

There are times when the following selection carries echoes for me of that well-known song, "The hills are alive with the sound of music," the sheer aliveness of Maria as she whirls in delight in the high Austrian hills that she loves so much, unaware of the puzzle she presents to the nuns in the convent where she is a novice. Listening to them singing their bewilderment catches some whisper of the aliveness of all that is.... How do you catch a cloud and pin it down? How do you hold a moonbeam in your hand? How do you keep a wave upon the sand?

The great danger... the trap into which one could fall, is to conceive of ultimate order as static. On the contrary, it is profoundly dynamic; the only image that we can ultimately find for this order is the dance of the spheres.... We are invited to attune ourselves to that harmony to which the whole universe dances. That order is simply the expression of the love that moves the universe, Dante's *l'amore che muove il sole e l'altre stelle* [the love that moves the sun and the other stars]. But the fact is that while the rest of the universe moves freely and gracefully in cosmic harmony, we humans don't. The obstacle which we must overcome is attachment, even the attachment to our own effort. Asceticism is the professional approach to overcoming attachment in all its forms. Our image of the dance should help us understand it. Detachment, which is merely its negative aspect, frees our movements, helps make us nimble. The positive aspect of asceticism is alertness, wakefulness, aliveness.

—*LH*, 11

Q: What do you see America needing spiritually?

Brother David: This ties in with the ecological question, which is intimately connected with the religious question nowadays. The core of every religious tradition is the mystical tradition, and mysticism is the experience of limitless belonging. That means limitless belonging to God, if you want to use that term, but also to all humans, to all animals, to all plants — that's at the core of the mystical tradition. And since the mystical tradition is at the core of religion, that sense of belonging is both ecological and religious.

Why would we do something about our environment? Because we belong here; this Earth is our home, our family. We have a responsibility toward it. Religion and ecology are deeply connected. For many people who wouldn't be caught dead in any church of any denomination, that ecological rightness is their religion, and I think that's perfectly valid. But also for many people who are Christians or Jews or Muslims or whatever else they may be, deep ecology is a genuine expression of their religious creed. In answer to your question, then, what is most urgently needed in American spirituality today is an ecological awakening. That would be the most appropriate religious gesture for today, it would require all the virtues that religion implies — faith, hope, love, sacrifice — and it's urgent. Unless this spiritual awakening takes place, we're lost.

At this point the number one offender is the military, with its economic ramifications. A fraction of the money we're spending on arms could deliver the whole world from hunger and pollution. And the military is the world's worst polluter, not only in the roundabout way of taking money that could be used to save the environment, but in that the money itself is spent on polluting the world. Think of the nuclear arsenal, all the planes and submarines and so on.

— From an interview with Richard Smoley,
Gnosis Magazine, Summer 1992

Nothing gives you more joy than when your heart grows wider and wider and your sense of belonging to the universe grows deeper and deeper. — WCS, 84

If we think of the Earth Household as our heavenly Father's "own and greater being," this will make us look at every pebble, every burr, every wood louse with reverence — and act accordingly. It will cause love to take its likes and dislikes as lightly as true faith takes its beliefs and true hope its hopes.... We all belong together. — GHP, 187

There is something intriguing about the image of a circle-dance. Just visualize it for a moment. As long as you stand outside of the circle, it will always seem to you that those nearest to you are going in one direction, those farthest away in exactly the opposite one. There is no way of overcoming this illusion except by getting into the circle. As soon as you hold hands and become one of the dancers, you realize that all are going in the same direction. The moment I brought up this image in my talk, I saw that the audience caught on. It was one of the great moments in my life — a peak experience, an experience of limitless belonging, a taste of the Now that does not pass away. Looking out over this assembly of the world's religions, I could almost hear an AMEN arising from many hearts.

God is the faithfulness at the heart of all things, faith is our response to that faithfulness, and the one-word expression of that faith is AMEN. From the core of our being (the Christ in us) we say Amen to Faithfulness (to God un-manifest), and saying AMEN is faith in action (the action of the Holy Spirit). Thus the very word AMEN reverberates with overtones of God as Trinity.

What else could dancers in the great circle-dance sing?

"Amen, Amen — and sing it again — Amen!"

—DTW, 174–75

MODERN SPIRITUAL MASTERS
Robert Ellsberg, Series Editor

Already published:

Dietrich Bonhoeffer (edited by Robert Coles)
Simone Weil (edited by Eric O. Springsted)
Henri Nouwen (edited by Robert A. Jonas)
Pierre Teilhard de Chardin (edited by Ursula King)
Anthony de Mello (edited by William Dych, S.J.)
Charles de Foucauld (edited by Robert Ellsberg)
Oscar Romero (by Marie Dennis, Rennie Golden,
   and Scott Wright)
Eberhard Arnold (edited by Johann Christoph Arnold)
Thomas Merton (edited by Christine M. Bochen)
Thich Nhat Hanh (edited by Robert Ellsberg)
Rufus Jones (edited by Kerry Walters)
Mother Teresa (edited by Jean Maalouf)
Edith Stein (edited by John Sullivan, O.C.D.)
John Main (edited by Laurence Freeman)
Mohandas Gandhi (edited by John Dear)
Mother Maria Skobtsova (introduction by Jim Forest)
Evelyn Underhill (edited by Emilie Griffin)
St. Thérèse of Lisieux (edited by Mary Frohlich)
Flannery O'Connor (edited by Robert Ellsberg)
Clarence Jordan (edited by Joyce Hollyday)
G. K. Chesterton (edited by William Griffin)
Alfred Delp, S.J. (introduction by Thomas Merton)
Bede Griffiths (edited by Thomas Matus)
Karl Rahner (edited by Philip Endean)
Sadhu Sundar Singh (edited by Charles E. Moore)

Pedro Arrupe (edited by Kevin F. Burke, S.J.)

Romano Guardini (edited by Robert A. Krieg)

Albert Schweitzer (edited by James Brabazon)

Caryll Houselander (edited by Wendy M. Wright)

Brother Roger of Taizé (edited by Marcello Fidanzio)

Dorothee Soelle (edited by Dianne L. Oliver)

Leo Tolstoy (edited by Charles E. Moore)

Howard Thurman (edited by Luther E. Smith, Jr.)

Swami Abhishiktananda (edited by Shirley du Boulay)

Carlo Carretto (edited by Robert Ellsberg)

John XXIII (edited by Jean Maalouf)

Jean Vanier (edited by Carolyn Whitney-Brown)

The Dalai Lama (edited by Thomas A. Forsthoefel)

Catherine de Hueck Doherty (edited by David Meconi, S.J.)

Dom Helder Camara (edited by Francis McDonagh)

Daniel Berrigan (edited by John Dear)

Etty Hillesum (edited by Annemarie S. Kidder)

Metropolitan Anthony of Sourozh (edited by Gillian Crow)

Frank Sheed & Maisie Ward (edited by David Meconi, S.J.)